Religious Education in Steiner-Waldorf Schools

Religious Education

in Steiner-Waldorf Schools

EXTRACTS FROM RUDOLF STEINER'S
LECTURES AND MEETINGS

Edited by

HELMUT VON KÜGELGEN

TILDE VON EIFF

Floris Books

Translated by Johanna Collis
First published in German under the title
Zur religiösen Erziehung
by Bund der Freien Waldorfschulen, Stuttgart

First published in English in 2000
by Steiner Waldorf Schools Fellowship Publications
as *Towards Religious Education*

Second edition copyright © 1997 Bund der Freien Waldorfschulen, Stuttgart
English version © 2000, 2014 Steiner Waldorf Schools Fellowship Publications

Second edition published in 2014 by Floris Books in association
with the Steiner Waldorf Schools Fellowship

All rights reserved. No part of this publication may be
reproduced without the prior written permission of
Floris Books, 15 Harrison Gardens, Edinburgh
www.florisbooks.co.uk

British Library CIP Data available
ISBN 978-178250-041-4

Printed in Great Britain
by CPI Group (UK) Ltd, Croydon

Contents

	Foreword to the English edition	7
1.	Religion in Education	9
2.	The Inauguration of Religion Lessons and Religious Services	42
3.	The Curriculum and Methods for Different Ages	71
4.	Division of the Religion Lessons into Class Groups and Weekly Lessons	129
5.	Selecting Religion Teachers	132
6.	How the Religion Lessons Relate to Denominational Lessons	141
7.	The Sunday Services	165
8.	How the Religion Lessons and Services Relate to the Christian Community	176
	References	187
	Bibliography	188

Foreword to the English edition

This careful collection of quotations from Rudolf Steiner's lectures, together with articles by pioneer religion teachers documents the beginning and development of the independent religion lessons and the services as an integral part of Waldorf education.

In Germany the practice was (and still is) that mainly Protestant and Catholic clergy came into schools to give religion lessons. When the first Waldorf School was founded in Stuttgart for the children of workers of the Waldorf Astoria cigarette factory, there were many children whose parents did not belong to any denomination. However, there was a demand for non-denominational religion lessons, and to meet this demand Rudolf Steiner inaugurated the independent Christian religion lessons and then the Sunday Services for children.

In Steiner Waldorf schools in Britain and some other countries the independent religion lessons are the only religion lessons taught, which makes it all the more necessary that the nature of these lessons is sensitively discussed with the parents at the outset. Experience has shown that such conversations, when handled with the respect fo freedom inherent in our education, allow parents who are adherents of different forms of religion to welcome such a universally human approach to religion.

It is for this reason that not only religion teachers, but all teachers of Steiner Waldorf schools will find inspiration and guidance in this book. By pointing to religiosity as an essential quality of human nature and the importance therefore of it nurture to the whole human being, Rudolf Steiner has returned religion to its rightful place in education. The English edition opens this important material to colleagues all over the world, strengthening us further in our understanding and enthusiasm for educating children and young people in a way which will enable them to meet their tasks in life.

This book was first published in 2000 and the excerpts and quotations are from translations which were available then. Since then there have been new translations of Steiner's educational and other lectures, so there are sometimes differences in the exact wording of the quotations in this book and those of currently available lecture translations.

Karla Kiniger
Edinburgh
September 2013

1. Religion in Education

From lectures by Rudolf Steiner

The Renewal of Education

Basle, April 23, 1920

I should now like to draw your attention to the fact that our religious ideas, including those which we use for our religious instruction in schools, have all been passed down to us as our traditional heritage. But why should people be afraid of renewing their religious ideas? Simply because anything which has come directly from the spiritual worlds is suspect today. One prefers to cling to inherited forms, because, when searching for the new, one has to face a great void. The fear of this void is justified because as the human being today approaches his twenty-seventh or twenty-eighth year, his inner spiritual life, which up to this time was awakened through physical development, simply dies away. If inherited religious ideas were not echoing within us at least unconsciously or instinctively, our inner lives would be turned into mere deserts. Unless we adhered to some traditional religious beliefs, our soul-life, after the twenty-eighth year, would become desolate and barren. We must recognise and admit this objective fact of human development. Figuratively speaking one could say that mankind is becoming younger, not older, because in his passive development the human being matures at an ever younger age. The Greek developed body, soul and spirit passively until he was in his thirties, but the human being of today is able to develop his soul and spirit at this age only if he is spiritually active. As modern people's traditional religious views are gradually declining, they will feel more and more an inner coldness which they can overcome only by finding something else to uplift their soul. However, a purely intellectual approach will never satisfy such inner needs. Already during early childhood the intellect begins to have a negative effect which can be overcome only by a spurring of the will. The fact is that mankind, today, is capable of physical development only up to the twenty-seventh or twenty-eighth year and that any impulse towards a further development in older age must come from spiritual sources.

Basle, April 26, 1920

To do this, we first of all need to have a clear conception of what the human being in his wholeness really is. Nowadays people are of the opinion that thinking can be taught by instructing the growing child, step by step, in logical sequence, because they cannot observe the part thinking plays within the general pattern of human nature. I must admit that during the six decades of my life so far, I have used every opportunity to make just such observations. If one watches the growing human being and compares his early stages with those of his older age, one can detect certain interconnections which remain hidden to the untrained eye and which stretch across the various phases of his life. I should like to give an example which illustrates such links in human life with almost proverbial clarity.

If one observes children who, by right up-bringing, have developed a natural reverence for the grown-ups in their surroundings, and if one follows them through their various stages of life, one can discover that their feelings of reverence and devotion in childhood are gradually being transformed during the years leading to old age. As adults such persons may have a healing effect upon their fellow human beings so that by their mere presence, or through the tone of their voice, or perhaps by a single glance they can spread inner peace to others. Their presence can be a blessing because as children they have learnt to venerate and to pray in the right way. No hands can bless in old

1. RELIGION IN EDUCATION

age, unless in childhood they have been folded in prayer. Such metamorphoses of childhood qualities into later life follow quite definite patterns.

Basle, May 4, 1920

If the child is educated with loving care, supported by his sense of authority, and if he learns to develop his feeling and willing in dependence on the adult guide, his educator and teacher, then his own independent feeling and willing will be born at the right moment, namely at puberty. Children can rightly develop their feeling and willing only under the guidance of authority. If they are allowed to develop their own independent will prematurely, especially if what one could call certain secret functions of will intervene too early, damage for the rest of their lives will ensue. And if they are tempted to subject moral and religious impulses to their own judgments too early, they will make a premature contact with the finer organisations of their will.

I have to reaffirm that, up to the time of puberty, the child should learn to develop his moral and religious attitude under the moral and religious guidance of his teacher's authority. Only at puberty does the soul and spiritual life of the adolescent become sufficiently freed from the physical body for us to begin to allow him to make his own judgments.

Soul Economy

Dornach, December 25, 1921

If you observe humanity's attitude towards the world in past ages, you will find that in ancient times religion was never looked upon as mere faith – this only happened in later times – but that religions were based on direct experience and on insight into the spiritual worlds. The knowledge thus gained was considered to be as real as are the results of our modern natural-scientific investigations. Only in subsequent ages was knowledge confined to what is sense-perceptible and, consequently, supersensible knowledge was relegated to the religious realm.

And so the illusion came about that anything pertaining to metaphysical existence could be only a matter of faith. Yet, as long as religions rested on supersensible knowledge, this knowledge bestowed great power, affecting even the physical nature of the human being. Our modern civilization is not able to generate this kind of moral strength for the human being today. For when religion has become only a matter of faith, it loses power, it can no longer work right down into man's physical constitution. Though this is instinctively felt nowadays, its importance is not recognized. This instinctive feeling and searching for revitalizing forces has found an outlet which has become a distinctive feature of our civilization and which belongs to all that we call sports.

Religion has lost the power of strengthening the human physical constitution. Therefore an instinctive urge has arisen in people to gain access to such a source of strength by outward, physical means only. As life tends towards polarization, we find that human beings instinctively want to substitute the loss of invigoration, previously drawn from their religious experiences, by cultivating sportsmanship. I have no wish to harangue against sports. Neither do I wish to belittle their positive aspects. In fact I feel confident that these activities eventually will develop in a healthy manner. Nevertheless it must be said that sport will take on an altogether different position in human life from that of today, where it is a substitute for religious experience. Such a statement may well appear paradoxical, but truth, today, is paradoxical because modern civilization has drifted into so many cross-currents.

Dornach, January 7, 1922

However, are we really able to offer the growing child something that carries weight in a subject which is being debated so much today? Are we in a position to lead young people into Christianity while theologians are arguing more and more about the real being of Christ? Should it not be our task to find ways of helping each individual to relate him or herself to Christianity in freedom? We must not impart accepted dogmas or fixed formulae in our ethical and religious instruction, but we must learn to nurture the divine and spiritual element that lives in the human soul. Only then shall we guide the child rightly, and without impinging on his inner freedom, towards his eventual choice of his own religious denomination. Only then will pupils be saved from inner uncertainties on discovering that one grown-up is a member of the High Church while another may be a Puritan. We must succeed in enabling our pupils to get hold of the real essence of religion. Likewise, through the cultivation of the three moods of soul, gratitude, love and duty, we must succeed in allowing morality to develop freely in the child's soul instead of trying to inculcate it by means of set moral precepts.

This problem lies at the very heart of the social question and all talking about it or working in the social field will depend on our being able to provide the right basis for the moral education of the young. A significant part of the whole social question is simply a question of education.

It was only possible to present a few rough outlines of the moral and religious aspect of Waldorf education which we have been studying during the last few days. If our educational aims are rooted in a true knowledge of man, and as long as we realize that we must refrain from introducing dogmas, theories, or moral obligations into our teaching, we shall finally succeed in laying the right foundations for the moral and religious life of our pupils.

The Spiritual Ground of Education

Oxford, August 19, 1922

The way of thinking with which the teacher approaches his task must begin with reverence for the mysterious being of the child – reverence and gratitude go together here. There is only one mood in relation to the child which gives us the right impulses for educating and teaching him, and that is the religious mood.

We have religious feelings in many connections. We have religious feelings with regard to the flowers in a meadow when we let them work on us as creations of the divine-spiritual world order. We feel the same towards the lightning as it flashes among the clouds when we sense that it has its place in the divine-spiritual world order. This is how, above all, we must feel when, out of the deep womb of the world order, we are confronted in the child by something that gives us the highest possible revelation of what the world is. This mood provides us with one of the most important impulses in our educational methods.

The methods of education are different from methods used in dealing with things that are not filled with the spirit. The methods of education are founded on the way the teacher does everything out of religious, moral impulses. We can even have these feelings when faced with a child who has a bad character, for then our mood is one of tragedy rather than antipathy.

Some might say – since we are so frightfully objective even about unimportant things – that nowadays it is inappropriate to approach with religious feelings a fractious child who is making a proper nuisance of himself. They might ask why they should feel tragic when faced with a child who is making such a nuisance of himself. In our so frightfully objective age some parents even

1. RELIGION IN EDUCATION

admit that their child is a nuisance, whereas in former times it was not customary to do such a thing, since parents in those days regarded all their own children as 'well behaved'. This was a better mood to cultivate than what we have today.

Nevertheless, if as a gift from the divine-spiritual world order, in fact as a case of the highest revelation of that world, we are asked to teach a child who is difficult to bring up, this can certainly lead us into a mood of tragedy. By experiencing this tragedy we are helped to overcome the hazards and snags we encounter in the art of education.

If we can welcome even a fractious child, if we can feel the tragedy of it and if we can generate our impulse for action out of this very tragedy, then we shall experience an appropriate gratitude towards the divine world order through comprehending even this nastiness as something divine, though we might find such comprehension rather complicated to achieve.

...

Having welcomed that child, and having trained him through love to do what we want to educate him to do up to the age of puberty, we shall then be able to experience this growing human being in the right way by allowing him to stand beside us in freedom as our equal. If we are then in a position which requires us to educate such an individual still further, we shall be able to do so by confronting this now free being directly from intellect to intellect. By educating the child in this way, by not violating what should unfold freely of its own accord, but instead by allowing the spirit to wake up stage by stage through what one does as the teacher, we enable this youngster, when he reaches puberty, to experience the awakening of his own being. And this moment of awakening becomes the source of a strength that will be with him for the rest of his life ...

The three golden rules of education and teaching, which should make up the whole attitude and impulse of every teacher's work, grasped not merely intellectually but by the human being as a whole, must be:

- ◊ Religious gratitude towards a world that is revealed in the child, combined with
- ◊ An awareness of the child being a divine mystery which it is one's task as a teacher to release;
- ◊ Methods of education practised in love, through which the child can instinctively educate himself through us, so that we do not endanger his freedom even where it remains an unconscious element of organic growth.

Philosophy, Cosmology and Religion

Dornach, September 9, 1922

From this it is quite evident that we can succeed in renewing religious life on a basis of knowledge if we do not reject a method of cognition that can guide us into having a living experience of the spiritual human being and other spiritual beings. We have special need of this method of cognition precisely so that religious knowledge can be placed on a firm foundation. In the realm of religion, ordinary consciousness can at most systematize perceptions, clarify them, or formulate them into a doctrine, but it cannot find them. Without these perceptions, religion is limited to the traditional acceptance of what is derived from quite different soul conditions of humanity in earlier times. It is therefore limited to what would never satisfy a mind trained in modern science.

Therefore, if we are to base our religion upon knowledge, I must repeat for the third time something that I have already expressed today in regard to other areas of culture, but that must be expressed specifically for each separate area.

If, out of the spiritual needs of the present time, religious life is to be renewed and undergo vital stimulation, the spiritual life of our age must acknowledge fully conscious imaginative, inspired, and intuitive cognition. Especially for the religious area must this not only be acknowledged but, for a living religious content, our modern spiritual life must also apply these spiritual-scientific results in appropriate ways.

Dornach, September 10, 1922

What appears during waking life as religious longing, as religious awareness, is an after-effect of the soul's experience among the stars. What I have just described is the stage of our deepest sleep. In actual fact, it is out of our sleep that the we derive the religious feelings of our waking life

Just as religious life can be founded today in knowledge by means of the experience resembling that of primordial humanity, but permeated and formulated in intuitions by the fully developed consciousness, it can also be said that one can attain this religious knowledge if, through supersensible intuition, one is able to perceive and illuminate the condition of deepest sleep. For what rests in the depths of sleep was also the source of what preserved man's knowledge of the divine. Our day-consciousness is only a reflection of the potentialities for consciousness open to us. Likewise, what we bear within us as a natural religious feeling appears as a reflection of the glory and sublimity experienced by our soul, even if unconsciously, in the third stage of sleep.

We sink into the life of sleep not only to renew our tired body, or to gain the stimuli from sleep that our breathing and circulation need, or to acquire from the spiritual world the other impulses we need. What permeates us with religious feeling penetrates to the soul's surface, to the region of day-consciousness, from the profound depths through which human soul life streams during sleep.

One might say that as we live a philosophical life during the first stage of sleep, similar to that of earliest childhood – however paradoxical that may sound to present-day consciousness – and as in the second stage we live a cosmological life, so, in the third stage, we live a life of being permeated with divinity. From this third stage of sleep, we must then return to daytime consciousness.

Dornach, September 15, 1922

With the entrance of Christianity into human evolution, religious consciousness has therefore changed, for this consciousness is the earthly after-image of what man must experience as permeation with God in the spiritual world between death and a new birth. In all respects we are led by modern initiation science to a deeper comprehension of Christology. Therefore, we can speak of a renewal of religious consciousness by means of an anthroposophic insight, just as we have spoken in the past few days of a renewal of philosophy, which turns into a living philosophical science; likewise, we spoke of a deepening of cosmology through the inclusion of the insight into the higher worlds that can only be attained by means of intuition and inspiration. Through enhancement by anthroposophy, a renewal of religious consciousness, which only then will become a fully conscious Christian awareness, can be attained for the whole of mankind. Anthroposophy would like to contribute to the further rightful development of Christianity; this is meant in the sense that it does not want to become a new religion, but wants to help in the development of the Christian religion that came into the world through the Mystery of Golgotha. This Christian religion has in itself the power to develop further, and anthroposophy wishes to understand this in the right way and be a true aid in this further development.

So in these lectures I have sought to describe for you how philosophy, cosmology and religious knowledge are to be fructified by anthroposophy. Naturally, knowledge of religion is not religion. Religion can also be experienced if you devote yourself with your heart and inner being in an open-minded way to what intuitive knowledge communicates, for the heart and inner being can understand it. Therefore, the renewal of religious knowledge can bring about a new deepening of religious life.

1. RELIGION IN EDUCATION

Awakening to Community

Stuttgart, January 30, 1923

So we may say that anthroposophy begins in every case at the scientific level, calls art to the enlivening of its concepts, and ends in a religious deepening. It begins with what the head can grasp, takes on all the life and colour of which words are capable, and ends in warmth that suffuses and reassures the heart, so that man's soul can at all times feel itself in the spirit, its true home. We must learn, on the anthroposophical path, to start with knowledge, then to lift ourselves to the level of artistry, and to end in the warmth of religious feeling.

The Child's Changing Consciousness

Dornach, April 17, 1923

Now it would be natural to assume it must surely be deep love that motivates a child to imitate one particular person. But if one looks at how love shows itself in later life, even in the case of a very loving person, one will come to realize that by saying, 'The child chooses out of love,' one has not fully appreciated what is actually happening. For in reality the child chooses to imitate out of an even higher motive than that of love. The child is prompted by what in later life one might call religious or pious devotion. Although this may sound paradoxical, it is nevertheless so. The child's entire sentient-physical behaviour in imitation flows from a physical yearning to become imbued with feelings found in later life only in deeply religious devotion or during participation in a religious ritual. This attitude of soul is strongest during the child's earliest years and it continues, gradually declining, up to the change of teeth. The physical body of a newborn baby is totally permeated by an inner need for deeply religious devotion. What in later life we call love is just a weakened form of this pious and devotional reverence.

One could say that up to the change of teeth the child is fundamentally an imitative being. But – and here I must ask you not to misunderstand what I am going to say, for sometimes one has to resort to unfamiliar modes of expression in order to characterize something that has become alien to our culture – the kind of inner experience that pulses through the child's imitation like its very life blood, this is religion in a physical-bodily garment. Up to the change of teeth the child lives in a kind of 'bodily religion'. We must never underestimate the delicate influences – one could also call them imponderable influences – which, only through a child's powers of perception, emanate from the environment, summoning forth an urge to imitate. We must on no account underestimate this most fundamental and important aspect of the child's early years. Later on we shall see the great significance this has for both the principles and practical methods of education.

Dornach, April 20, 1923

Every education is self-education, and as teachers we can only provide the environment for the child's own self-education. We have to provide the most favourable conditions in which, through our agency, the child can educate itself in accordance with its own destiny.

This is the attitude the teacher should have towards the child, and it can be developed only through an ever-growing awareness of this fact. For people in general there may be many kinds of prayers. Over and above these there is this special prayer for the teacher: 'Dear God, make that I, as far as my personal ambitions are concerned, quite obliterate myself. And Christ, make true in me the Pauline words, "Not I, but Christ in me".' This prayer, addressed to God in general and to Christ in particular, continues: '... that the Holy Spirit may hold sway in the teacher.' This is the true Trinity for the teacher.

1. RELIGION IN EDUCATION

A Modern Art of Education

Ilkley, August 5, 1923

Knowledge that thus draws the creative activity of the universe into itself can flow directly into art, and this same path from knowledge to art can be extended and continued. It was so continued through the powers of the old imaginative knowledge, which also found the way, without any intervening abyss, into the life of religion. He who applied himself to this kind of knowledge – primitive and instinctive though it was in early humanity – did not feel it as something external, for in his knowing and thinking he felt that the divinity of the world lived in him, that the creatively divine passed over into artistic creativeness in man.

Then the way could be found, however, to raise what man in art impressed on matter to a still higher consecration. The activity which he made his own as he embodied the divine-spiritual in outer material substance he could then extend into acts wherein he was fully conscious that he, as a human being, was expressing the will of the divine powers of the world. He felt himself pervaded by divine creative power, and as the path was followed from the elaboration of material substance to human action, art passed over, by way of ritual, into the service of the divine. Artistic creation became service of God.

What is done in the ritual represents the consecrated artistic deeds of ancient humanity. Artistic deed was raised into ritual deed, the glorifying of God through matter to devotion to God through the ritual of the service. And as man thus bridged the abyss between art and religion there arose a religion in full harmony with knowledge and with art. Albeit primitive and instinctive, this knowledge was none the less a true picture, and as such it could lead human deeds to become, in the acts of ritual, a direct portrayal of the divine.

In this way the transition from art to religion was made possible. Is it still possible in our present-day mode of knowledge? The ancient clairvoyant perception had revealed to man pictorially the spiritual in every creature and process of nature, and through the surrender and devotion of human beings to the spirit within the nature-processes, the all-swaying, all-creative spirituality of the cosmos passed over into the ritual.

...

All true religions have sprung from inspiration. True, the early form if inspiration was not so conscious as that to which we must now attain, yet it was there instinctively, and rightly do the religions trace their origin back to it. Such faiths as will no longer recognize living inspiration and revelation from the spirit in the immediate present will have to be content with tradition. But such faiths lack all the inner vitality, all direct motive-power of religious life. This motive-power and vitality must be re-won, for only so can our social organism be healed.

I have shown how man must regain a knowledge that passes by way of art to imagination and thence to inspiration. If he re-acquires all that flows down from the inspirations of a spiritual world into human consciousness, true religion will once again appear. And then intellectual discussion about the nature of Christ will cease, for once again it will be known – as it can indeed be known through Inspiration – that the Christ was the human bearer of an actual divine being who had descended from the spiritual world into earthly existence. Without supersensible knowledge there can be no understanding of the Christ. If Christianity is again to be deeply rooted in humanity, the path to supersensible knowledge must be rediscovered. Inspiration must again impart a truly religious life to mankind in order that knowledge – derived no longer merely from the external observation of nature – may find no abyss dividing it alike from art and religion. Knowledge, art, religion – these three will then be in harmony.

Primeval man counted on the presence of God in human deeds when he made his art a divine office, and when he shared in the fire that can glow in the heart of the human being when the divine will pervades the acts of ritual. And when the path from outer, objective knowledge to inspiration is found once again, religion

1. RELIGION IN EDUCATION

will flow directly from inspiration and modern human beings will be able – as were primeval human beings – to stand within a God-given morality.

In those ancient days a human being felt, 'If I have the ritual, if I have the divine service, if the ritual is in the world and I am woven into it, then my inner being is filled so that in the whole of my life and not only where the ritual is celebrated I can make God present in the world.'

To be able to make God present in the world – this is true morality. Nature cannot lead man to morality. Only that which lifts him above nature, filling him with the divine-spiritual – this alone can lead man to morality. Only that intuition which comes over man, when through the religious life he places himself in the spirit, can fill him with real inmost morality at once human and divine.

The attainment of inspiration thus rebuilds the bridge once existing instinctively in human civilization between religion and morality. As knowledge leads upwards through art to the heights of supersensible life, so, through religious worship, spiritual heights are brought down to earthly existence, so that we can fill this existence with the impulse of an essential, primal, direct morality actually experienced by man.

Thus will man himself become in truth the individual bearer of a life pulsed through by morality, filled with an immediate moral impulse. Morality will then be a creation of the individual himself, and the last abyss between religion and morality will be bridged. The intuition in which primitive man stood as he enacted his ritual will be re-created in a new form, and a morality truly corresponding with modern conditions will arise from a modern religious life.

We need this for a renewal of our civilization. We need it in order that what today is mere heritage, mere tradition, may spring again into original life. This primordial impulse is necessary for our complicated social life that is threatening to spread chaos through the world. We need a harmony between knowledge, art, religion, and morality. In a new form we need this way which leads from the earth and along which we win our knowledge, passing through inspiration and through the arts to the direct life in the supersensible, to a taking hold of the supersensible, so that we can again lead down into social life on the earth the supersensible which we have felt in religion and transformed into will.

Only when we see the social question as one of morality and religion can we grapple with it in its full depths, and this we cannot do until the moral and religious life arises from spiritual knowledge. If human beings again achieve spiritual knowledge, they will be able to do what is needed, to link their further evolution to an instinctive origin. They will find what must be found for the healing of humanity: harmony between science, art, religion and morality.

Ilkley, August 8, 1923

Hence it can be said that if we would reach the human being from out of thought in a living way, if we would bring the spirit in its livingness to human beings, we must enter into the artistic. If we would bring feeling, the spiritual feeling, the feeling spirit to human beings, we must not merely set about this with an artistic mood as in the former case, but also with a religious mood. For the religious mood alone can penetrate to the reality of the spirit.

Education between the seventh and fourteenth year, therefore, can only be carried on in the truly human sense when it is carried on in an atmosphere of religion, when it becomes almost a sacramental office – not, of course, in a sentimental, but in a truly human sense.

So we see how what the human being does comes streaming in when he brings life and soul to his otherwise abstract thinking, thinking that merely arises from the association of ideas. We see how he finds the way to an apprehension of man within the religious life. Art and religion are thus united with education.

Thus the way becomes clear from the question of the pupil to that of the teacher when we realize that pedagogy should become so practical, so clear and so living a knowledge that the teacher can only be a true educator of youth when he is able inwardly to become a thoroughly artistic, a thoroughly religious person.

Ilkley, August 12, 1923

So, just as the earliest initiates had explained *Ex Deo nascimur*, and those who came later *In Christo morimur*, the initiation wisdom which bears within itself a future life of conscious spiritual knowledge, a life leading to a deepening of religious feeling, to a divine consciousness – this initiation wisdom would lead human beings once again to know that the Christ who passed through the Mystery of Golgotha is the Logos, weaving and working through the cosmos. And inasmuch as human beings will gradually grow to be conscious of their cosmic existence, the initiation science that is intended to inaugurate a spiritual Christology in the truest sense (as well as an art of education, for instance, in a narrower sphere) will strive to bring a religious mood into the practical life it ever seeks to serve. 'Out of God we are born as physical human beings,' 'In Christ we die' – that is to say, 'As a soul, we live.' To these truths initiation science will ever strive to add the third: 'When we press forward through the new initiation to the Spirit, then even in this earthly life we become alive in the Spirit.' We experience an awakening whereby all our life is bathed in the light of true religion, and in the light of a moral goodness proceeding from inner piety. In short, this new initiation science endeavours to supplement the answers to the first and second riddles of initiation as expressed in the *Ex Deo nascimur* and in the *In Christo morimur*, while at the same time it solves them anew and restores them to the soul of man. It endeavours to bring afresh and in full clarity to the human heart, this other truth – a truth that will awaken the Spirit in man's heart and soul: in the understanding of the living Spirit, we ourselves, in body, soul and spirit, shall be re-awakened: *Per Spiritum Sanctum reviviscimus*.

Ilkley, August 17, 1923

On the basis of these principles a bridge may be built to moral and religious education. I have already spoken of this and need only add today that everything depends upon giving all the teaching and all bodily, all gymnastic exercises in a form which will make the child feel: my bodily nature is a revelation of spirit and the spirit would fain pour creatively into my body. The child must never feel a separation between spirit and body.

The moral and religious elements will then live truly in his life of feeling. The great thing to bear in mind is that between the change of teeth and puberty we must not inculcate morality and religion into the child by means of catechism-precepts but by working upon his feeling and perception through our own authority in connection with this period of life. The child must learn to delight in goodness and to abhor evil – to love the good and hate the wicked.

In the history lessons, great historical figures and the impulses connected with the different epochs can be presented in such a way that moral and religious sympathies and antipathies will unfold in the child. And then we achieve something of supreme importance.

After puberty, when the child has reached his fifteenth or sixteenth year, a change takes place in his inner nature, leading him from dependence upon authority to his own sense of freedom and hence to the faculty of independent judgment and insight. Here is something that must claim our most watchful attention in education and teaching. If, before puberty, we have awakened the child's feeling for good and evil, for what is and is not divine, these feelings will arise from his own inner being afterwards. His understanding intellect, insight and power of judgment are uninfluenced; he can now form independent judgments from out of his own being.

If we start by telling the child that he ought to do this and ought to do that, it all remains with him through his later years and then he will always be thinking that such and such a thing is right and such and such a thing is wrong. Convention will colour everything. Now in true education today, the human being should not stand within the conventional but have his own judgment even about morality and religion, and this will unfold naturally if it has not been prematurely engaged.

At the Waldorf School we allow the child of fourteen or fifteen to find his own feet in life. We put him really on a par with ourselves. He unfolds his judgment but he still looks back to the authority which we represented, and retains the affection he had for us when we were his teachers. His power of judgment has not been fettered if we have merely worked upon his life of feeling. And so, when the child has reached the age of fourteen or fifteen, we leave his nature of soul and spirit in freedom and, in the higher classes, appeal to his own power of judgment and insight. This freedom in life cannot be achieved by inculcating morality and religion in a dogmatic, canonical fashion but by working simply and solely on the child's powers of feeling and perception at the right age – the period between the change of teeth and puberty. The great thing is to enable the human being to find his place in the world with due confidence in his own power of judgment.

He will then sense himself to be a true human being because his education has been truly and completely human. If someone has been unfortunate enough to have lost a leg or an arm, he cannot feel himself a complete human being; he is conscious of mutilation. Children of fourteen or fifteen, educated according to modern methods, begin to be aware of a sense of mutilation if they are not permeated with the qualities of moral judgment and religious feeling. Something seems to be lacking in their humanity. There is no better heritage in the moral and religious sense than to bring children up to regard the elements of morality and religion as such an integral part of their being, that they do not feel themselves wholly human if they are not permeated with morality, warmed through and through by religion.

This can only be achieved if we work, at the proper age, on the life of feeling and perceptive experience alone, and do not prematurely give the children intellectual conceptions of religion and morality. If we do so before the twelfth or fourteenth year, we are bringing children up to be sceptics – men and women who, instead of healthy insight, in later life develop scepticism in regard to the dogmas inculcated into them – to begin with, scepticism in thought (the least important), but then scepticism in feeling, which makes them defective in feeling. And finally there will be scepticism of will which brings moral error in its train.

The point is this: our children will be brought up only to be sceptics if we present moral and religious ideals to them dogmatically; such ideals should only come to them through the life of feeling. Then, at the right age they will awaken their own free sense of religion and morality which will then become part of their very being. And they feel that only this can make them fully human. The great aim at the Waldorf School is to bring up free human beings who know how to direct their own lives.

Supersensible Knowledge as a Demand of the Age

Vienna, September 29, 1923

Permit me to introduce here a special example. Out of everything that fails to satisfy us in that which confronts us today also in the educational life, what concerned us when the Waldorf School was to be founded in Stuttgart on the initiative of Emil Molt was to answer the question as to how a human being ought really to be educated. In approaching this task, we addressed this question to the supersensible world of which I am here speaking. I will mention only briefly what sort of purposes had then to be made basic.

First of all, the question had to be raised, 'How is a child educated so that he becomes a real human being, bearing his whole being within himself but also manifesting his whole being in the ethical-religious conduct of life?' A genuine knowledge of the human being in body, soul and spirit was necessary for this.

...

1. RELIGION IN EDUCATION

What I have just introduced to you might be indicated in a picture if we say that, in relationship to the universe as well, the human being may be so educated that he may transmute into forces of blessing in high old age the forces of reverence of his tender childhood. Permit me to indicate in a picture what I mean. No one will be able to open his hands in blessing in old age who has not learned in tender childhood to fold his hands in reverent prayer.

This may indicate to us that in such a special case a life task, education, may lead to an ethical-religious attitude of mind; may indicate how that which our hearts and minds and our wills, become as a result of entering livingly into spirit-knowledge may enter with vital reality into our conduct of life, so that what we develop otherwise, perhaps, only in an external and technical way shall become a component part of our moral-religious conduct of life. The fact, however, that instruction and education in the Stuttgart Waldorf School, and in the other schools which have arisen as its offshoots, have been brought into such an atmosphere does not by any means result in a lack of attention to the factual, the purely pedagogical; on the contrary, these are given full consideration. But the task of education has really become something here which, together with all its technique of teaching, its practice of instruction and everything methodical, at the same time radiates an ethical-religious atmosphere over the child. Educational acts become ethical-religious acts, because what is done springs from the most profound moral impulses. Since the practice of teaching flows from a teacher-conscience, since the God-given soul nature is seen in the developing human being, educational action becomes religious in its nature. And this does not necessarily have any sentimental meaning but the meaning may be precisely what is especially necessary for our life, which has become so prosaic: that life may become in a wholly unsentimental sense a form of divine service to the world, as in the single example we have given of education, by reason of the fact that spiritual science becomes a light illuminating the actions of our life, the whole conduct of life. Since supersensible knowledge leads us, not to abstractions, but to human powers, when these forms of knowledge gained through supersensible cognition simply become immediate forces of life, they can flow over, therefore, into our whole conduct of life, permeating this with that which lifts the human being above his own level – out of the sensory into the supersensible – elevating him to the level of a moral being. They may bring him to the stage where he becomes, in consecrated love, one with the spirit of the world, thus arriving at truly religious piety.

Indeed, this is especially manifest also in education. If we observe the child up to his seventh year, we see that he is wholly given over, in a physical sense, to his environment. He is an imitator, an imitative being even in his speech. And when we observe this physical devotion, when we observe what constitutes a natural environment of the child, and remains such a natural environment because the soul is not yet awake, then we feel inclined to say that what confronts us in a natural way in the child is the natural form of the state of religious consecration to the world. The reason why the child learns so much is that it is consecrated to the world in a natural-religious way. The human being separates himself from the world; and, from the seventh year on, it is his educational environment which gives a different, dimly sensed guidance to his soul. At the period of adolescence he arrives at the stage of independent judgment; then he becomes a being who determines his own direction and goal from within himself. Blessed is he if now, when freed from his sense organism, he can follow the guidance of thought, of the spirit, and grow into the spiritual just as he lived in a natural way while a child in the world – if he can return as an adult in relationship to the spirit to the naturalness of the child's feeling for the world! If our spirit can live in the spirit of the world at the period of adolescence as the body of a child lives in the world of nature, then do we enter into the spirit of the world in true religious devotion to the innermost depths of our human nature: we become religious human beings.

We must willingly accept the necessity of transforming ordinary concepts into living forces if we wish to grasp the real nature, the central nerve, of supersensible knowledge. Similarly, when we view the human being by means of what I described the last time as supersensible knowledge in imagination. When we become aware that what lives in him is not only this physical body which we study in physiology, which we dissect in the medical laboratory and thereby develop the science of physiology, when we see that a supersensible being lives in him which is beheld in the manner I have described, we then come to know that this supersensible being is a sculptor who works upon the physical body itself. But it is necessary then to possess the capacity of going over from the ordinary abstract concepts, which afford us only the laws of nature, to an artistic conception of the human being. The system of laws under which we ordinarily conceive the human physical form must be changed into moulded contents; science must pass over into art. The supersensible human being can not be grasped by means of abstract science. We gain a knowledge of the supersensible being only by means of a perception which leads scientific knowledge wholly over into an artistic experience. It must not be said that science must remain something logical, experimental. Of course, such a demand can be set up; but what does the world care about what we set up as 'demands'! If we wish to gain a grasp of the world, our process must be determined in accordance with the world, not in accordance with our demands or even with our logical thoughts; for the world might itself pass over from mere logical thoughts into that which is artistic. And it actually does this. For this reason, only he arrives at a true conception of life who – by means of 'perceptive power of thought' to use the expression so beautifully coined by Goethe – can guide that which confronts us in the form of logically conceived laws of nature into sculpturally moulded laws of nature. We then ascend through art – in Schiller's expression 'through the morning glow of the beautiful' – upwards into the land of knowledge, but also the land of reverent devotion, the land of the religious.

We then learn to know – permit me to say this in conclusion – what a state of things we really have with all the doubts that come over a human being when he says that knowledge can never bestow upon us religious and ethical impulses, but that these require special forces far removed from those of knowledge. I, likewise, shall never maintain, on the basis of supersensible knowledge, that any kind of knowledge as such can guide a human being into a moral and religious conduct of life. But that which really brings the human being into a moral and religious conduct of life does not belong in the realm of the senses: it can be investigated only in the realm of the supersensible. For this reason a true knowledge of human freedom can be gained only when we penetrate into the supersensible. So likewise do we gain real knowledge of the human conscience only when we advance to the sphere of the supersensible. For we arrive in this way at that spiritual element which does not compel the human being as he is compelled by natural laws, but permits him to work as a free being, and yet at the same time permeates him and streams through him with those impulses which are manifest in the conscience. Thus, however, is manifested to man that which he vaguely senses as the divine element in the world, in his innocent faith as a naive human being imbued with religious piety. It is certainly true that one does not stand in immediate need of knowledge such as I have described in order to be a religious and pious person; it is possible to be such a person in complete naivety. But that is not the state of the case, as history proves. One who asserts that the religious and ethical life of man must come to flower out of a different root from that of knowledge does not realize on the basis of historical evolution that all religious movements of liberation – naturally, the religious aptitudes always exist in the human being – have had their source in the sphere of knowledge as supersensible sources of knowledge existed in the prehistorical epochs. There is no such thing as a content of morality or religion that has not grown out of roots of knowledge. At the present time the roots of knowledge have given birth to scientific thinking, which is incapable, however, of reaching to the spirit. As regards the religious conduct of life, many people cling instead to traditions, believing that what exists in traditions is a revelation coming out of something like a 'religious genius'. As a matter of fact, these are the atavistic,

1. RELIGION IN EDUCATION

inherited traditions. But they are at the present time so faded out that we need a new impulse of knowledge, not working abstractly, but constituting a force for knowledge, in order that what exists in knowledge may give to the human being the impulse to enter even into the conduct of practical life with ethical-religious motives in all their primal quality.

This we need. And, if it is maintained on the one hand – assuredly, with a certain measure of justification – that the human being does not need knowledge as such in order to develop an ethical-religious conduct of life, yet it must be maintained, on the other hand, as history teaches in this respect also, that knowledge need not confuse the human being in his religious and his ethical thinking. It must be possible for him to gain the loftiest stages of knowledge, and with this knowledge – such, naturally, as it is possible for him to attain, for there will always remain very much beyond this – to arrive at the home in which he dwelt by the will of God and under the guidance of God before he had attained to knowledge. That which existed as a dim premonition, and which had its justification as premonition, must be found again even when our striving is toward the loftiest light of knowledge. It will be possible then for knowledge to be something whose influence does not work destructively upon the moral conduct of life; it may be only the influence which kindles and permeates the whole moral-religious conduct of life. Through such knowledge, however, the human being will become aware of the profounder meaning of life – about which it is permissible, after all, to speak: he will become aware that, through the dispensation of the mysteries of the universe, of the whole cosmic guidance, he is being willed by the spirit, as he deeply senses; that he can develop further as a being willed by the spirit; that, whereas external knowledge brings him only to what is indefinite, where he is led into doubt and where the unity which lived within him while he possessed only naive intimations is torn apart, he returns to what is God-given and permeated of spirit within himself if he awakens out of the ordinary knowledge to supersensible knowledge.

Only thus can that which is so greatly needed by our sorely tested time really be furthered – a new impulse in the ethical-religious conduct of life: in that, just as knowledge has advanced up to the present time from the knowledge of vague premonition and dream to the wakeful clarity of our times, we shall advance from this wakeful clarity to a higher form of waking, to a state of union with the supersensible world. Thus, likewise, will that impulse be bestowed upon the human being which he so imperatively requires especially for the renewal of his social existence at this time of bitter testing for humanity in all parts of the world – indeed, we may say, for all social thinking of the present time. As the very root of an ethical-religious conduct of life understanding must awaken for the fact that the human being must pass from the ordinary knowledge to an artistic and supersensible awakening and enter into a religious-ethical conduct of life, into a true piety, free from all sentimentality, in which service to life becomes, so to speak, service to the spirit. He must enter there in that his knowledge strives for the light of the supersensible, so that this light of the supersensible causes him to awaken in a supersensible world wherein alone he may feel himself to be a free soul in relationship to the laws of nature, wherein alone he may dwell in a true piety and a genuine inwardness and true religiousness as a spirit man in the spirit world.

The Essentials of Education

Stuttgart, April 9, 1924

If we understand what is happening from the perspective of a child, we find that the soul-being of the child – with everything brought from pre-earthly life from the realm of soul and spirit – is entirely devoted to the physical activities of human beings in the surroundings. This relationship can be described only as a religious one. It is a religious relationship that descends into the

1. RELIGION IN EDUCATION

sphere of nature and moves into the outer world. It is important, however, to understand what is meant by such terms.

Ordinarily, one speaks of 'religious' relationships today in the sense of a consciously developed adult religion. Relevant to this is the fact that, in religious life, the spirit and soul elements of the adult rise into the spiritual element in the universe and surrender to it. The religious relationship is a self-surrendering to the universe, a prayer for divine grace in the surrender of the self. The soul and spirit are yielded to the surroundings.

To speak of the child's body being absorbed by the environment in terms of a religious experience thus seems like we are turning things around the wrong way. Nevertheless, it is a truly religious experience – transposed into the realm of nature. The child is surrendered to the environment and lives in the external world in reverent, prayerful devotion, just as the eye detaches itself from the rest of the organism and surrenders to the environment. It is a religious relationship transferred to the natural realm.

If we want a picture, or symbol, of the spirit and soul processes in the adult's religious experience, we should form a real idea in our souls of the child's body up to the change of teeth. The life of the child is 'religious', but religious in a way that refers to the things of nature. It is not the *soul* of the child that is surrendered to the environment, but the blood circulation, breathing activities, and the nutritional process through the food taken in. All of these things are surrendered to the environment – the blood circulation, breathing, and digestive processes pray to the environment.

These expressions may seem contradictory, but their very contradiction represents the truth. We must observe such things with our whole being, not theoretically. If we observe the struggle unfolding in the child before us – within this fundamental, natural religious element – if we observe the struggle between the hereditary forces and what the individual's forces develop as the second human being through the power brought from pre-earthly life, then, as teachers, we also develop a religious mood. But, whereas the child with the physical body develops the religious mood of the believer, the teacher, in gazing at the wonders that occur between birth and the change of teeth, develops a 'priestly' religious attitude. The position of teacher becomes a kind of priestly office, a ritual performed at the altar of universal human life – not with a sacrificial victim to be led to death, but with the offering of human nature itself, to be awakened to life. Our task is to ferry into earthly life the aspect of the child that came from the divine spiritual world. This, with the child's own forces, forms a second organism from the being that came to us from the divine spiritual life.

Pondering such things awakens something in us like a priestly attitude in education. Until this priestly feeling for the first years of childhood has become a part of education as a whole, education will not find the conditions that bring it to life. If we merely try to understand the requirements of education based on external observations of a child's nature, at best we accomplish a quarter education. A complete educational method cannot be formulated by the intellect alone, but must flow from the whole human nature – not merely from the part that observes externally in a rational way, but the whole that deeply and inwardly experiences the secrets of the universe.

Few things have a more wonderful effect on the human heart than seeing inner spirit and soul elements released day to day, week to week, month to month, year to year, during the first period of childhood. We see how, beginning with chaotic limb movements, the glance filled with rapture by the outer, the play of expressions that do not yet seem to belong to the child, something develops and impresses itself on the surface of the human form that arises from the centre of the human being, where the divine spiritual being is unfolding in its descent from pre-earthly life. When we can make this divine office of education a concern of the heart, we understand these things in such away that we say, 'Here the Godhead who has guided the human being until birth is revealed again in the impression of the human organism; the living Godhead is there to see; God is gazing into us.' This, out of the teacher's own individuality, will lead, not to something learned by rote, but to a living method of education and instruction, a method that springs from the inner being.

This must be our attitude to the growing human being; it is essential to any educational method. Without this fundamental attitude, without this priestly element in the teacher (this is said, of course, in a cosmic sense), education cannot be continued. Therefore, any attempt to reform the methods of education must involve a return of the intellectual element, which has become dominant since the fourteenth century, to the domain of soul and feelings, to move toward what flows from human nature as a whole, not just from the head. If we look at the child without preconceptions, the child's own nature will teach us to read these things.

Stuttgart, April 11, 1924

In the moral realm we allow pleasure in the good and displeasure in the evil to grow; we allow the religious element, which was originally natural in the child, to awaken in the soul. In the depths, however, between the change of teeth and puberty there develops the seed and foundation – something already was present – that becomes free understanding after the age of puberty. We prepare a free understanding of the world that includes the religious and moral spheres. It is great when a person can recognize how pleasure and displeasure were experienced as a permeation of the whole life of feeling as the moral qualities of good and evil during the second period of life.

Then the impulse arises: the good that pleased you – this is what you must do! And what displeased you, you must not do. This principle of morality arises from what is already present in the human I, and a religious devotion toward the world arises in the spirit, which had been a thing of nature during the first period, and a thing of the soul during the second. The religious sense – and will applied to the religious impulse – becomes something that allows human beings to act as though God were acting in them. This becomes the expression of the I, not something imposed externally. Following puberty, if the child has developed in accordance with a true understanding of the human being, everything seems to arise as though born from human nature itself.

...

At this point, let me mention something I have often spoken of. A true teacher must always keep in view all of human life. A teacher must, for example, be able to see the wonderful element that is present in many older people, whose very presence brings a kind of blessing without much in the way of words; a kind of blessing is contained in every gesture. This is a characteristic of many people who stand at the threshold of death. From where does this come? Such individuals have this quality because, during childhood, they developed devotion naturally. Such reverence and devotion during childhood later becomes the capacity to bless. We may say that at the end of earthly life, people cannot stretch out their hands in blessing if they have not learned to fold them in prayer during childhood. The capacity for blessing when one grows old and comes near the threshold of death originates with folding one's hands in prayer with reverent, childhood devotion. Everything visible as a seed in the child will develop into good or evil fruit as the person progresses farther along in earthly life. And this is something else that must be continually within view in order to develop a genuine teaching method based on real life in education.

The Roots of Education

Berne, April 14, 1924

The way a child breathes or digests in the more delicate and intimate processes of breathing or digesting reflects the actions of those around the child.

Children are completely surrendered to their environment. In adults the only parallel to such devotion is found in religion as

1. RELIGION IN EDUCATION

expressed through the human soul and spirit. Religion is expressed in spiritual surrender to the universe. The religious life unfolds properly when, with our own spirit, we go beyond ourselves and surrender to a spiritual worldview – we should flow out into a divine worldview. Adult religious life depends on emancipating soul and spirit from the physical body, when a person's soul and spirit are given up to the divine spirit of the world. Children give up their whole being to the environment. In adults, the activities of breathing, digestion, and circulation are within them, cut off from the external world. In children, however, all such activities are still surrendered to their environment, and they are therefore religious by nature. This is the essential feature of a child's life between birth and the change of teeth; the whole being is permeated with a natural religious element, so to speak, and even the physical body maintains a religious mood. But children are not surrounded only by beneficial forces that inspire religious devotion in later life. There are also spiritual forces that are harmful, which come from people around children and from other spiritual forces in the world. In this way, this natural religious element in a child's physical body may also be exposed to evil in the environment – children can encounter evil forces. And when I say that even a small child's physical body has a religious quality, I do not mean that children cannot be little demons! Many children are little demons, because they have been open to evil spiritual forces around them.

Our task is to overcome and drive out such forces by applying methods appropriate to our time. As long as a child is an imitative religious being, admonitions do no good. Words can be listened to only when the soul is emancipated to some extent, when its attention can be self-directed. Disapproving words cannot help us deal with a small child. But what we ourselves do in the presence of the child does help, because when a child sees this it flows right in and becomes sense perception. Our actions, however, must contain a moral quality.

If, for example, someone who is colour-blind looks at a coloured surface, he may see only gray. An adult looks at another person's actions also in this way, seeing only the speed and flow of the gestures. We see the physical qualities but no longer see the moral qualities of the person's actions. A child, on the other hand, sees the moral element, even if only unconsciously, and we must make sure that, while in the presence of children, we not only never act in a way that should not be imitated, but never think thoughts that should not enter their souls.

Berne, April 16, 1924

With regard to religion, we must be clear that young children are naturally religious. At the change of teeth, when the soul and spirit become more free of the body, this close relationship with nature falls away, and thus what was formerly natural religion must be lifted to a religion of the soul. Only after puberty does religious understanding arise, and then, once the spirit has become free, what was formerly expressed in imitation of the father or mother must be surrendered to the invisible, supersensible forces. Thus, what has always been present in the child as a seed gradually develops in a concrete way. Nothing is grafted on to the child; it arises from the child's own being.

Here is an extraordinary fact you can verify for yourselves. With all relatively rational people – and nearly everyone is rational these days (and I mean that seriously) – you find that people have been educated only to be rational, only to work with their heads, and no more. To educate the whole person is not as easy. You only have to read what very sensible people have written about education, and you repeatedly encounter this sort of statement: 'Nothing should be presented to a child from outside; but what is already there should be developed.' You can read that everywhere, but how is it done? That is the question. It is not a matter of establishing principles. Programmatic principles are easy to come by, but what matters is to live in reality. This is what we must aim for, but we will find ourselves nearly overwhelmed by the difficulties and dangers in our path.

Thirty, forty, or a hundred people can sit down together

1. RELIGION IN EDUCATION

today and draft treatises on the best methods for teaching and education and other recommendations, and I am convinced that in most cases they do it very cleverly. I am not being ironic – our materialistic culture has reached its zenith. Everywhere societies are being established and principles elaborated. In themselves, these are splendid, but they accomplish nothing. That is why the Waldorf School came into being in such a way that there were no set principles or systems – only children and teachers. We have to consider not only the individuality of every single child, but the individuality of every single teacher as well. We must know our teachers. It is easy to draft rules and principles that tell teachers what to do and not do. But what matters is the capacities of the individual teachers, and the development of their capacities; they do not need educational precepts, but a knowledge of the human being that takes them into life itself and considers whole persons in a living way. You see, our job 'must always be *development*, but we must know where to look for what we wish to develop. We must link religious feeling – and later, religious thinking – with imitation during the first stage of childhood, and moral judgment during the second.

2. The Inauguration of Religion Lessons and Religious Services

Religion lessons and the Sunday Services
in Steiner Waldorf Schools

Herbert Hahn

In the preparatory talks about the inner structure of the new Waldorf School which Rudolf Steiner conducted during the spring and summer of 1919, he initially made no mention of special religion lessons that would accord with the spirit of Waldorf education. In fact he had once expressed the view that owing to the central importance in Waldorf education of an image of the human being rooted in the spirit, every lesson would do justice to what would otherwise have to be cultivated in lessons specifically about religion.

As early as the autumn of 1919, however, the timetable included two 'non-denominational' religion lessons per week for each class. This change of plan, which surprised some people, came about – as did all the steps Rudolf Steiner took in life – because the need for it had become obvious to him. The reason was that considerable groups of Protestant and Catholic parents were keen for their children to have religion lessons in their own faith in addition to the general curriculum of the school.

Rudolf Steiner complied with this wish coming from the majority of parents by agreeing that these religion lessons should be 'extra-territorial'. In other words, the school would make the necessary classrooms available but would neither bear

2. RELIGION LESSONS AND RELIGIOUS SERVICES

educational responsibility for the lessons nor interfere with them in any way.

In the process of making the necessary arrangements, it turned out that there was a group of pupils requiring neither Protestant nor Catholic nor any other religious instruction. Most of these were the children of workers and other employees in the Waldorf-Astoria cigarette factory, which was not only the instigator of the school but also supplied the core of the first pupil intake.

Since the need for separate religion lessons was to be taken into account, Steiner did not want the children of non-religious parents to be placed in a special position through having no religion lessons at all. So for those whose parents expressly wished it he established non-denominational Christian religion lessons that came to be called 'independent religion lessons' in the sense that they were independent from confessional views. They had the sole aim of equipping the children with living religious forces for their later activities in life. The task he set was to depict and unfold the great fundamental truths of Christianity in a free way.

The lessons were to be given by teachers at the Waldorf School or other friends, which meant that in the method of teaching Steiner was able to take account of certain aspects which arise from the view of the human being held by spiritual science. As with all the other subjects taught in the Waldorf School, this did not mean that the lessons would be used for 'instruction in anthroposophy'. It was necessary to ensure that a misunderstood 'anthroposophical tendency' be radically excluded from the living stream of education developed in the school, and any serious investigation will show that this was indeed the aim. While on the one hand these lessons were to be closely linked to the methods used in the education as a whole, on the other hand they were not to stand out from those other, denominational, lessons. This meant that these religion lessons, too, would also have to be treated as being 'extra-territorial'.

The first teachers called upon by Rudolf Steiner to give these lessons in the autumn of 1919 (probably October) were Friedrich Oehlschlegel for Classes 5 to 8, and I myself for Classes 1 to 4.

The children in question in each of these two groups of classes were divided into two large groups, one with the younger and one with the older children in each case. This meant that both Oehlschlegel and I only had two religion lessons to give per week. The overall methodical basis for the two age-groups was given by Steiner in the meeting of September 26, 1919.

On November 3, 1919, a few weeks after the introduction of the new lessons, a parents' evening took place in the Waldorf School for the parents of the children who attended them. As far as I remember, only one subject was discussed at that meeting, namely whether some kind of Sunday celebration could be arranged for those children. In the main it was Emil Molt, the founder of the Waldorf School, who spoke up on behalf of this wish that was coming to life among the parents. After various suggestions had been put forward by those present, Oehlschlegel and I were asked to consider the matter further. We were to work out some concrete suggestions and discuss these with Dr Steiner on his next visit to Stuttgart.

Experience clearly showed both Oehlschlegel and me that these suggestions coming from the parents were in keeping with a growing need. The lessons we gave called for something more inward that would go beyond mere instruction and have the character of a celebration of some kind. But any ideas we came up with as to the form this celebration might take confronted us with a dilemma. Everything we thought of seemed to be no more than a poor imitation of traditional ways, or else it was too subjective. We considered a reading from the gospels, for example, or a short talk, or perhaps the depiction in eurythmy of the relevant verse from the *Calendar of the Soul*.

We were greatly relieved, therefore, when Dr Steiner returned to Stuttgart during the Christmas period and readily agreed to explore our concerns with us. We told him about the parents' evening and recounted the ideas we had so far considered. Patiently, and with his kindly, serious smile, he listened to what we had to say. The only remark he made was in connection with the idea of performing the weekly verse in eurythmy. 'In eurythmy?' he queried. 'But

2. RELIGION LESSONS AND RELIGIOUS SERVICES

eurythmy is a profane art! I should have to inaugurate forms for a eurythmy suitable to be a *sacred art*.'

There followed, as far as I remember, a pause in the conversation. Then Rudolf Steiner appeared to start, and he called out with much emphasis, 'This will have to be a proper ritual [*ein Kultus*]!' We looked at him in surprise. Still with emphasis, he continued, 'But it will be exceedingly difficult to set it up. If we introduce it, it will have to be totally "taboo"!'

After another short pause he continued in his normal voice, 'But surely we shall be able to set it up; it would have to be set up in such a way as to show that it *is* something.'

And after a further pause for thought: 'If we are able to do this, it will at the same time link on to our esoteric work that had to be broken off because of the war.'

Rudolf Steiner then said that he would look into what possibilities there were for taking up a ritual, a *Kultus*, of this kind, and that he would keep us informed. That was the end of the meeting.

As regards the historical development of our work, it is important to point out that the idea of a ritual had never come up in Oehlschlegel's or my considerations. The suggestions we had made to Rudolf Steiner did not go beyond the idea of a Sunday act of worship. The suggestion as to the objective form of the ritual came exclusively from him.

There was no further conversation on this matter. A few days later Dr Steiner gave us his answer in the form of the text for the first Sunday Service. We copied it down, and Oehlschlegel kept the original. Dr Steiner had pointed to Frau Bertha Molt and Frau Hertha Kögel as helpers, and together with them we set about getting ready for the first service. The chief necessity was to prepare the room.

Oehlschlegel and I had been able to have a further conversation with Dr Steiner about all the details in the arrangement of the room. He drew the exact shape of the altar and said that the altar and the whole room should be in red. The candle-holders were to be black, and there should be seven. They should be arranged with an obtuse angle at the front with the smallest at the point and the two largest at each end. On the wall behind the altar should be Leonardo da Vinci's coloured sketch of Christ's head for the Last Supper which is kept in the Brera Gallery in Milan; the frame was to be blue.

Indications about the chairs for the helpers to the right and left of the altar were only given by Dr Steiner later, when the Offering Service was instituted. Originally there were no chairs. Dr Steiner gave no indications as to the orientation of the altar or the room as a whole.

I remember Dr Steiner being especially warm and welcoming during the conversation in which he told us all these details. He gave us to understand that he shared our sense of something great and important taking place through the inauguration of these services. He accompanied us to the door with unforgettable cordiality once the conversation was over.

The actual beginning of the services was to bring about a drastic turning-point in my own destiny. In January 1920, Friedrich Oehlschlegel suddenly decided to embark on a journey to the United States of America. As a German American he believed he saw possibilities in the United States for awakening a strong interest in the idea of a threefold social organism. He set off on this trip without informing Dr Steiner and under circumstances some of which remain a riddle to this day. It was ill-starred. Oehlschlegel fell so ill in America that he was forced to retire permanently from the association of the Waldorf School. Thus I found myself faced with the difficult task of carrying the actual introduction of the services by myself.

The first service took place on February 1, 1920. A great many children took part in a festive mood. Thereafter it fell to me for over a year to hold the services alone, first the Sunday Service, and subsequently also the Christmas Service and Youth Service given by Rudolf Steiner. This was because after Oehlschlegel's departure Dr Steiner did not immediately appoint a new religion teacher. So I also had to take on Oehlschlegel's group for religion lessons (Class 5 to 8). The next teacher to join me for the religion lessons was Ernst Uehli. He was followed by Wilhelm Ruhtenberg. Adolf Arenson and Sigismund von Gleich also temporarily took on some of the groups for religion lessons. Soon after his arrival from Vienna, in February 1920, Dr Karl Schubert also participated in a Sunday Service, but he only became a religion teacher several years later.

When he happened to be in Stuttgart Dr Steiner frequently came to the Sunday Services. This occurred for the first time on February 29, 1920. Occasionally he was accompanied by Frau Steiner. Otherwise he was most insistent that the services, including those who participated, should remain strictly an internal matter for the school. He regarded it as natural and desirable that apart from the appropriate children all the members of the College of Teachers should participate. Apart from this, participation was to be restricted to the parents of the children in question or, in the case of boarders, the representatives of the parents. Requests by others to come to the services were not infrequent, but Dr Steiner always firmly refused. On one occasion he stated that the foundations for the inner care of these 'ritual' services was a conscientious protection of their setting.

Since it had not been possible to discuss with Dr Steiner every last detail regarding the setting up of the services and the room, I asked him several times after his early visits whether he was satisfied with the way in which we had carried out his suggestions, or whether he thought it would be right to do one thing or another differently. Repeatedly he said, 'This is fine,' or, 'It is quite alright like this.' Thus even in the matter of these details we have a confirmation that is objectively valid.

When I asked him about a gospel text for the beginning of the services he suggested the first 14 verses of the Gospel of John. For a long time this text was read each Sunday. Later on he recommended selecting the gospel texts loosely in accordance with older collections of Bible stories.

As is also borne out by his initial conversation with Oehlschlegel and me, he regarded the introduction of the services as a matter to be treated with the utmost care and responsibility. Something of this concern also showed in his attitude during the early months of 1920. Some time later, in one of his meetings with the teachers, he said in effect, 'As regards the Sunday Services, I can imagine all kinds of attitudes towards them. However, I can also understand that those who are directly concerned with them have feelings which resemble those of the early Christians as they descended into the catacombs.' From then onwards we experienced how Dr Steiner regarded the Sunday Services as an objective fact which formed a unity with the religion lessons.

Dr Steiner gave the Christmas Service during the Christmas period of 1920 after I had asked him a question about such a possibility. This Service was held for the first time on December 25 of that year. It was followed in 1921 by the Youth Service on Palm Sunday. Two years later, after receiving enquiries from pupils in what was at that time the top class, he also gave us the text of the Offering Service. This was held for the first time on Palm Sunday, March 25, 1923, by Dr Karl Schubert, Dr Maria Röschl and myself.

As I have already stressed, once they had been introduced, Dr Steiner regarded the services as an integral part of the religion lessons at the Waldorf School. He did not want the religion lessons to be given at Waldorf schools or other institutions *unless* the services were going to be held as well. He even once called the services the third religion lesson. Of course he did not mean by this that children attending the religion lessons should be obliged to go to the services. But as the number of teachers giving the religion lessons increased, he made sure that none of these gave the lessons without also holding the services, and vice versa.

It was noticed that this aspect of the services played a critical role in his selection of teachers for the religion lessons. He was often heard to say, 'Well, so-and-so would be quite capable of giving the religion lessons, but it would not work as far as the services are concerned!' We should emphasize once again at this point that Dr Steiner found it perfectly acceptable to call upon suitably capable members of the Anthroposophical Society to give the religion lessons even if they did not belong to the College of

Teachers at the school or even if they were not teachers at all. The extraordinarily tentative, delicate manner in which he felt his way towards each new nomination to join the group of religion teachers shows what a huge human and spiritual responsibility attached to the development of these lessons.

Although this needs to be strongly emphasized on the one hand, it is on the other hand also necessary to pre-empt any supposition that Rudolf Steiner handled the imponderable aspects in a way the might foster some kind of mysticism or false esoteric aspirations. As with everything else he did, he dealt with them in an atmosphere of spiritual clarity and objectivity that left and indeed made others entirely free. His words were simple, sober and very often tinged with the humour which he addressed as a sign of something healthy in spiritual matters. Those who were called upon by him gained an impression of being allowed to serve in freedom – no more and no less.

After his basic talk in 1919 as to the method,[1] Rudolf Steiner later gave many other indications regarding the material suitable for the religion lessons. At the end of this article I still very much want to emphasize the following. Many of the suggestions Dr Steiner gave arose in specific situations and were directed to specific teachers. The conversations with him – usually brief – that arose in these situations showed that Dr Steiner liked to tie in with whatever the teacher in question had just been working on and was therefore particularly filled with at that moment. He frequently enquired, 'What have you been working on lately?' Then he would surprise the person by saying, 'Well, in a suitable form that is just what you can tackle with the children.' He did not mean by this that the teacher should inundate the children with anthroposophical content. But he considered the best material to be whatever was alive and therefore objective in the teacher's mind so long as it was presented in a manner suited to the children's age. Thus, as with all the other subjects taught in the Waldorf School, he attached the greatest value to each teacher's own creative input.

This is why we never systematize any of the materials and

methods we collect. Those who carry and cultivate these – in the highest sense of the word – '*independent* religion lessons' are thus unceasingly called upon to use their own initiative.

The Offering Service

Maria Lehrs-Röschl

This essay by Maria Lehrs-Röschl is included here because of its historical significance. Ongoing comprehensive study is called for in our search for the meaning of the esoteric substance entrusted to us by Rudolf Steiner through the Offering Service. [Editors]

In the discussion we religion teachers had with Rudolf Steiner on December 9, 1922, we brought up, among other matters, the request by Johanna Wohlrab, a pupil in what was then the top class in the school, for those in the upper classes who had been participating in the Youth Service for nearly two years to be given a Sunday Service that would go beyond the Youth Service. I remember that we considered this question to be at least premature and were in no way expecting Rudolf Steiner to react positively.

Yet he listened with particular attention to this suggestion and said that it had far-reaching significance and he would think further about it. He would not want to include an actual mass among the Services connected with the religion lessons, but 'something *like* a mass could be possible'.

In March 1923 Rudolf Steiner was in Stuttgart and gave the text for the Offering Service to Dr Hahn, Dr Schubert and me. We were to copy it out. On Palm Sunday, March 25, we three held this service for the first time for the pupils of Class 11 and the teachers.

After this, some colleagues approached us with the request to repeat the Offering Service for the teachers alone. We were unsure as to whether this service, like the others, was intended solely for the pupils (including teachers and parents). In fact we were almost certain that this was the case. I was asked to put this question to Rudolf Steiner.

I formulated my question in words that expressed my assumption that it would not be appropriate to hold the Offering Service except for the pupils. Rudolf Steiner looked at me with wide open eyes (I was familiar with this gesture of surprised, slightly disapproving astonishment) and said, 'Why not? This Service can be held wherever there are people who want it.'

So on Good Friday, March 30, 1923, we held the Offering Service for the first time for teachers alone, without pupils. Subsequently the Service was repeatedly held in this way, especially as a memorial for colleagues who had died and at the annual reunions of former pupils, although hitherto only for those who had earlier participated in the religion lessons.

To understand more about this service we must try to understand what Rudolf Steiner *meant* by 'something like a mass'. There are various possible interpretations, so that one might take them to signify something that comes either before or after the mass in its line of development, something that is either below or above the mass. It would be easy to let subjective interpretations creep in, which would be inconsistent with the objective development of this kind of ritual service. The words 'like a mass' state that we are concerned on the one hand with something which is identical with a mass but which on the other hand is not absolutely identical with a mass.

In earlier statements Rudolf Steiner said that in its origins the Catholic mass could be traced back to ancient mysteries which had continued on from Persia and Egypt, and that in those streams it had taken on an especially popular form.[2]

Pupils of those mystery schools were first of all told about the creation of the world and the human being, and his significance in the world – how the world spirit poured itself into every manifestation of creation in the kingdoms of nature, and how the human being was a conflux of all creation: a microcosm within a macrocosm. How man, who had brought darkness into this pure world through his passions and imperfections, could attain the transformation of his being by offering his lower nature for catharsis, thus reaching union with his divine origin – this was taught to the pupils at another stage through *services*.

The mass arose out of the services of those mysteries. To this day the Christian mass unfolds in the four stages of the Gospel, Offertory, Transubstantiation and Communion. This is how the Offering Service is built up, so in this it is the same as the mass. It is in no way the same, but only similar, to the mass as regards the substances in the Offertory and the Transubstantiation. It would be incorrect to suppose that there were no substances in the Offering Service. They are present as the body and blood of the human being who in his *consciousness* wants to imbue himself with an inner experience of the sacrifice of Christ on Golgotha, in keeping with the words

> May the devotion of our souls
> Lead into this offering place
> The experience of Christ's offering for mankind.

Regarding what occurs on the altar, Rudolf Steiner pointed very clearly already in 1909 and 1911 to this change as being in the line of development of the service of the mass. He first mentioned this in his discussion of the Transubstantiation in the lectures on the Gospel of John given in Kassel. He pointed out that we are still only at the beginning of the development of Christianity. The future of this development will consist in our reaching a full comprehension of the fact that through the Mystery of Golgotha Christ created a new centre of light in the midst of the earth. Thus Christ's words on instituting the Last Supper (Communion) express the fact that he has made the earth into his body. This is realized ritually by the use of the substances of bread and wine.

> And those who are able to grasp the true meaning of these
> words of Christ create for themselves thought images that

2. RELIGION LESSONS AND RELIGIOUS SERVICES

attract the body and the blood of Christ in the bread and wine, and they unite with the Christ Spirit. In this way the symbol of the Lord's Supper becomes a reality. Lacking in our hearts the thought that unites us with Christ we cannot engender the force of attraction that draws the Christ Spirit to us at Holy Communion; but by means of such a thought form the attraction is generated. For those, then, who need the outer symbol in order to perform the spiritual act – that is, to unite with the Christ – Communion will be the way until such time as their inner strength will have so grown, and they are so permeated by the Christ, that they can dispense with the outer physical agency. *The Sacrament of Communion is the preparation for the mystical union with the Christ – it is the preparatory schooling.* That is the light in which we must see these things. And just as everything evolves from matter upward toward spirit under the Christian influence, so those things which existed primarily as a bridge must then grow and develop under the influence of Christ. *The Sacrament of Communion must rise from the physical to the spiritual plane if it is to lead to a true union with the Christ.*

One can do no more than hint at such matters, for only if they are received with a full sense of their sacred nature will they be rightly understood.[3]

In this as well as in the following passage, Rudolf Steiner's starting point was a remark about the approaching atomic age. In 1911, in the lecture cycle *From Jesus to Christ*, he discussed the exoteric path which can lead the human being to Christ via the Communion and the gospels. Then he stressed that in their endeavours on the inner path given by spiritual science, human beings can become sufficiently mature

> in their inner being not merely to experience thought-worlds, or worlds of abstract feelings and perceptions, but to permeate themselves inwardly with the element of the Spirit; thereby they will experience *the Communion in*

the Spirit; thereby thoughts, meditative thoughts, will be able to live in a human being; they will even be the very same, only from within outwards, as the symbol of the Holy Communion, the consecrated bread, has been from without inwards.

He continued by saying that in the future this path was to become an exoteric path for human beings.

But then all ceremonies will change, and that which formerly came to pass through the attributes of bread and wine will come about in the future through a spiritual Communion. The thought of the Sacrament, the Holy Communion, will remain, however.[4]

Taken together, these passages from 1909 and 1911 make it clear where the Offering Service is situated on the line of historical development: not *before*, but *after* the mass with bread and wine. It is not – as might have been presumed, seeing that it does not involve a transformation of substance – an earlier step, not a preparation for a mass with bread and wine. The bread and wine received by the human being are absorbed by the force which works to transform substance in the *unconscious* depths of his body and which, from there, can gradually bring about clarity and transformation in his consciousness. In contrast, communion in the spirit as experienced in the Offering Service, is a *deed of consciousness* which can become ever clearer and work right down into the physical body of the human being. The passages quoted clearly point to the Transubstantiation and Communion as given by Rudolf Steiner twelve years later in the Offering Service. In the continuation of the above quotation, he put forward, as a precondition for a Communion in spirit, that

> certain inner thoughts and feelings shall permeate and spiritualise our inner being – thoughts and feelings as fully *consecrated* as in the best sense of inner Christian development the Holy Communion has spiritualised

the human soul and filled it with the Christ. When this becomes possible – and it will become possible – we shall have progressed a stage further in evolution. And then we shall see the real proof that Christianity is greater than its external form.

The Offering Service provides the form for these consecrated thoughts that permeate and spiritualise our inner being. All we have to do is free ourselves of the prejudice which tells us that thoughts are only ever something abstract. The kind of thoughts depends on the one who is doing the thinking. Thoughts can become an *experience* strong enough to work formatively right down into the physical. This can happen through the Offering Service right into the body and blood of one who strives to reach the Christ.

Thanks to the image spiritual science gives us of the evolution of man and cosmos, the words of the Offertory given in the Offering Service, spoken with raised arms, and those spoken in reply by the one standing on the right, can widen out to embrace the thought of the *cosmic* biography of the being 'man'. Before us can stand the description of that time when the Sun departed from the Moon-bound Earth. Together with the Sun there departed from the earth that lofty being of the human 'I' whom we now call Christ. The hierarchical archetypal images of man departed also, leaving merely reflected images behind. This meant: in the service of cosmic evolution, the human being took upon himself the *sacrifice* of descending further into the darkness of the material world which was then forming – an event of evolution from which high spirit beings who did not want to follow the human being in this descent 'hid their faces'.

Our thoughts can penetrate even further back to a phase of evolution when *pre-Saturnine* humanity – which could have undergone a very lofty development without any descent into matter (though without an unfolding of the independent 'I') – entered into the cosmic cycle in order to tread this very path of physical laws.[5] It was this step which introduced

> Look upon the offering
> Of our manhood's being
> Of our body, imbued with soul
> Of our blood, imbued with spirit

that descent into the darkness of matter out of which we cannot find the possibility to ascend again without the power of Christ. Beings of a future world can arise if in the course of his evolution the human being can find the strength to bring into existence that 'fire of love which created being' which can work from man to God, and also from man to man.

Of course not every participant in the Offering Service will be able or want to make this connection to long past cosmic phases of humanity's path. All manner of experiences are possible in any kind of ritual service.

It is the *goal* that matters, for the goal is indeed effective. It is the goal of the Offering Service that we should unite with the 'I' of humanity in body and blood, right down to our physical being. That this goal is attainable in our present time was stressed by Rudolf Steiner in personal conversations, for example with Friedrich Rittelmeyer, who mentioned this in his book *Rudolf Steiner Enters My Life*, before going on to put on paper some important thoughts about the two kinds of Communion.

Thus the enquiry and expectation of that young girl were indeed of far-reaching significance. They provided Rudolf Steiner with the opportunity to give to humanity in the form of a ritual what he had already hinted at in 1909 and 1911.

Asked what the consequences were of having this ritual performed by people who were not ordained priests, Rudolf Steiner is said to have replied that he had taken the matter as far as was possible without ordained individuals. This reply is also far-reaching in its significance. There has always been in Christianity a longing for a lay priesthood, a longing that was frequently persecuted and finally made to disappear. Now Rudolf Steiner has sown the seeds for a revival which, depending on destiny, will be able to bear fruit in individual cases. This will be achieved by those who in their inner endeavour achieve ordination through their encounter with the highest Self, the Christ.

Introducing the services in curative education

Siegfried Pickert

At the Lauenstein [in Germany, home for children in need of special care] we began to hold the Sunday Service on August 9, 1925. Introducing the services into the curative work had been discussed with Dr Ita Wegman at the end of the 1925 Whitsun youth conference in Dornach. On behalf of the Executive Council she asked Dr Hahn to give us the texts and advise us in the early days. [Albrecht] Strohschein and I went to see Herbert Hahn in Stuttgart, where we participated in the service and received his advice and instructions on how to prepare the room and conduct the service. Herbert Hahn was simply the mediator in this matter, since our work actually stood under the auspices of the Medical Section. Initially I was asked (by Dr Wegman) to conduct the service, with Strohschein as doorkeeper. A short while after this Dr Hardt was asked to conduct the service, and later still Strohschein and [Franz] Löffler were asked (in about 1926). At the same time Dr Röschl began to hold the services at the Sonnenhof [another special care home in Arlesheim, Switzerland]. After she left Dornach, Dr [Julia] Bort and [Werner] Pache took on this role.

All this emanated directly from Dr Wegman, including the engagement of the doorkeepers at the Sonnenhof and Lauenstein. I did not pass on the services to other institutions on my own initiative before 1941 (when anthroposophical work was prohibited by the Nazis). We were of course in regular contact with Herbert Hahn and Karl Schubert. The inner precondition for the handling of this entire matter depended upon the existence of the Medical Section, whose the leader had played a major role in the original full Executive Council.

The services and religion lessons in Camphill

Anke Weihs

Although the following text was composed in the Camphill Schools in Scotland it can be regarded as generally, though not specifically, valid for all Camphill Schools. [The description is from 1971]

When Dr König came to Scotland to found a community working to care for and educate handicapped and disturbed children in the light of the curative education inaugurated by Rudolf Steiner, an essential element in his impulse was give the four services a central role in this new initiative.

At the very beginning Dr König introduced the Offering Service for special occasions. This service became a point of spiritual orientation and had a formative influence on the nascent community. It also provided the basis for the introduction of the other three services once the flow of children to Camphill had begun.

The Offering Service was and is held in the community of adults on the main festival days of the year or to mark specific internal events such as the death of a child or co-worker, or for occasions such as the internal conferences of the larger Camphill community. Individual co-workers are not obliged to participate, but those who do so are aware of its importance; and the community at large is conscious of its responsibility to protect and care for the Offering Service.

In some Camphill centres the Offering Service is attended by co-workers and the older pupils together.

A harmonious and fruitful relationship with the Christian Community has developed in some Camphill village communities for handicapped adults. This enables both the Offering Service and the Act of Consecration of Man to find their appropriate place within the religious life of the community.

The Children's Service [Sunday Service] has been held in Camphill since 1942. Quite early on it became a weekly Sunday event. All the children attend the service.

2. RELIGION LESSONS AND RELIGIOUS SERVICES

However, some seriously disturbed younger children may need a longish period of preparation prior to full attendance. Usually this takes the form of a gospel reading (John 1) and some lyre music immediately after the end of a Children's Service while the candles still burn on the altar and the room is still filled with the mood of the Service. After weeks, in some cases months, of individual preparation a very disturbed child can join in the service with the other children. With only a few exceptions the service proves to be a event during which the children can lay aside their difficulties and behavioural problems, becoming remarkably receptive to all that the service intends to bring them.

While Camphill was still small and restricted to a single location, the Children's Service used to be celebrated on St John's Day and at Michaelmas as well. But as the community grew and spread, other ways were found in which to celebrate these important spiritual milestones of the annual cycle.

When the pupils have reached their fourteenth birthday they are brought into the Youth Service on Easter Sunday. For the subsequent two years they continue to attend this service regularly.

The annual group of fourteen-year-olds in Camphill, Scotland, is relatively large. It is especially important for developmentally disturbed youngsters to cross the threshold from childhood to youth at the right time since this transition is not supported by a healthy biological development. For this reason, and after careful consideration, some of the youngsters therefore wait until Michaelmas to be introduced to the service.

Children with handicaps and disturbances need proper preparation for the important events in their lives. Therefore each group, those attending the Youth Service for the first time on Easter Day and those waiting until Michaelmas Day, are given special religion lessons for several weeks beforehand to help each one recognize the importance of this step at the beginning of his or her growing maturity. Introduction to the Youth Service is a community event accompanied by much anticipation on all sides, and many parents attend.

The Christmas Service is held on Christmas Day. In the Camphill Schools, where the children only go home for the holidays after Christmas, this service is also held again on the following Sunday. All the children including those who go to the Youth Service attend. The oldest pupils, who attend the Offering Service, sit with the co-workers.

In the Camphill Schools, Scotland, where there are 200 children and about 35 co-worker children, the following services are held every Sunday: the Children's Service five times, the Youth Service twice, and the Offering Service once for the oldest pupils. In Newton Dee, the neighbouring village community for handicapped adults, the Offering Service is also held every Sunday. Mostly the services are conducted by three people.

The number of services held each week in other Camphill centres depends on the numbers of children and other age groups. Where possible over-large groups are avoided.

Most Camphill centres have built special rooms specifically for the services. These are only otherwise used for Class Lessons or more intimate studies and meetings. In a curative setting the service cannot help but take on a centrally therapeutic significance. When a child with a severe handicap or disturbance, struggling to master his or her difficult destiny, manages to stand up straight in the Sunday Service and say, 'I will seek him' – even if speech is impaired – the teachers and therapists accompanying that child will recognize in this the healing power and effect of the Word, the Logos, and will know that the child is on the way to experiencing the meaning of human existence.

The services are a central healing force that brings order and direction to a more generally therapeutic and educational situation. This does not mean that they have to be slanted to fit a specific situation. They are quite simply an existential space in which the soul can find healing.

In the early days of Camphill – 1939 to 1942 – responsibility for the services in Camphill was carried by Dr König and his wife until a group was formed to share the growing responsibility necessary for the Services.

2. RELIGION LESSONS AND RELIGIOUS SERVICES

When the need arises to appoint new service holders, the group of service holders, after careful consideration and discussion, approaches a co-worker whose attitude towards the services has proved responsible and helpful. If this co-worker is willing to take on a further responsibility, he or she begins as a doorkeeper at the Children's Service and also takes on a group of children for religion lessons for about a year before holding a service for the first time. Efforts are made to let the Religion Teachers' Gremium know the names of the service holders in the Camphill centres.

The group of service holders meets weekly to discuss the services for the coming Sunday and to consider other matters in connection with the services.

The perennial question of how to translate the original text into other languages is a major concern in some groups of service holders in Camphill. At the annual conferences of the whole Camphill movement the service holders from the various centres meet to exchange experiences, for example as to what is involved in celebrating the services in South Africa where the seasons are reversed, and to discuss other matters to do with the services.

In a community that has been striving spiritually for nearly 33 years a great deal of artistic creativity has originated in the services. The architects Gabor Tallo and Joan Allan, for example, have built appropriate buildings in which the services can be held. Carlo Pietzner in the USA and Hermann Gross in Scotland have designed glass windows and paintings for the service rooms, and Christof Andreas Lindenberg has composed a large body of lyre music as well as songs and choruses for the services.

At the same time a number of individual customs have grown up around the services over the course of 33 years.

Some years ago, while Dr König was still alive, Herbert Hahn visited Camphill. On that occasion a number of questions regarding the holding of the services were clarified in a frank and warm discussion. For many years some of the service holders from the different Camphill centres have been participating in the meetings of religion teachers in Stuttgart and Dornach, which enables them to maintain fruitful contact with those responsible for the services both in the Steiner Waldorf movement and in curative education elsewhere.

Children living in communities that emphasize the importance of the annual Christian festivals experience a religious social education in a natural way. Apart from the general spiritual and cultural life of the community, all children in Camphill centres have a weekly religion lesson appropriate to their age group. The teachers base their general plan on Herbert Hahn's suggestions for religion lessons for healthy children.

For the aphasic, psychotic and deaf children, all of whom have a weakness where hearing the spoken word is concerned, special eurythmy performances and also puppet plays are prepared in which the intimate mood needed for imparting religious content can be generated. These special measures take place at the same time as all the other religion lessons and are treated as religion lessons.

As children with handicaps grow up, their religion teachers may well also find themselves 'travelling an extra mile' with them. Taking into account Rudolf Steiner's descriptions of the soul before birth perceiving the panorama of its imminent life and also experiencing its recently concluded life after death, teachers may well find themselves gently asking what such a child might have experienced before being born. We learn that the child now appearing in our midst, needing our compassion and protection, may possess exceptional qualities of courage, self-sacrifice and karmic insight.

There are moments when a religion teacher experiences a shimmer of ancient wisdom, experience and suffering in a pupil. In such moments he regards himself not as a teacher but as a midwife in the Socratic sense whose task it is to bring to the fore the child's inward spirituality and knowledge of the divine.

2. RELIGION LESSONS AND RELIGIOUS SERVICES

Establishment of the International Religion Teachers' Gremium

The 1951 Resolution

> concerning the appointment of religion teachers at schools belonging to the Bund der Freien Waldorfschulen [Association of Steiner Waldorf Schools, in the following simply 'Bund'] and concerning the administration of the texts of the 'ritual' services held in conjunction with the independent religion lessons.

In the autumn of 1919 the independent religion lessons at the Stuttgart Waldorf School were inaugurated by Rudolf Steiner as a sector which though linked with the spirit of the school was to be administered extra-territorially and cultivated out of anthroposophical responsibility. Between 1919 and 1923 Dr Rudolf Steiner gave the texts of four 'ritual' services to be held in conjunction with the religion lessons and to be cared for and passed on by a collegium of religion teachers which gradually came into being at the Stuttgart Waldorf School. These were the Sunday Service, the Christmas Service, the Youth Service, and the Offering Service.

The manner in which Steiner passed on these texts, and also the spiritual strictness, reserve and care with which he only very gradually enlarged the college of religion teachers, indicated that in their whole extent these matters have to do with things imponderable and of the highest spiritual responsibility.

Events of history and destiny which came into play very soon after Rudolf Steiner's death, but especially after 1933, caused the administration of the functions and obligations connected with the religion lessons to be taken up to a great extent by separate centres of initiative which in part had no contact with one another. In this important field which Rudolf Steiner once characterized as the heart of the education work, the overview and uniformity essential for the protection and cultivation of high spiritual matters entrusted to us thus became endangered.

At a meeting during the 1951 autumn conference of the Bund der Freien Waldorfschulen, religion teachers in member schools therefore, in the presence of a representative of the college of religion teachers from the Vrije School in The Hague, decided to take an initiative to protect the extension and cultivation of the religion lessons and the services connected with them by means of a resolution freely entered into.

With regard to the origin of the religion lessons and their tasks they therefore resolved as follows, on behalf of the schools represented by them:

1. In resumption of a usage introduced by Rudolf Steiner, the college of religion teachers at the Stuttgart Waldorf School (Uhlandshöhe) is declared responsible for confirming new religion teachers at schools attached to the Bund. Suggestions for the nomination of new religion teachers shall – after contact with the internal teachers' meeting of the school in question – be passed to the Stuttgart college of religion teachers. At schools which do not as yet have a college of religion teachers, the internal teachers' meeting of the school in question shall consult with the Stuttgart college of religion teachers prior to making a specific suggestion.

As a matter of principle any person put forward shall be an anthroposophist who has been working in an anthroposophical setting for quite some time.

Only when the Stuttgart college of religion teachers has expressed its confirmation shall the person put forward as the new religion teacher in the school in question be considered to be appointed in that function.

The Stuttgart college of religion teachers for its part shall report to the Executive Council of the General Anthroposophical Society at Dornach regarding all teachers newly appointed as religion teachers within the Bund.

2. RELIGION LESSONS AND RELIGIOUS SERVICES

2. When a religion teacher takes on a function in connection with the Sunday Services, the relevant texts and instructions shall be handed to him or her personally by a member of the Stuttgart college of religion teachers or by a religion teacher appointed to do so by the college. The texts of the services shall be responsibly administered by the college of religion teachers at the Stuttgart Waldorf School. The texts are to be entrusted to the religion teacher only for the duration of his or her work or function in connection with the services.

The teacher receiving the service texts shall sign a declaration stating his or her agreement that when he or she ceases to be a religion teacher, or in the case of death, the texts shall be returned to the college of religion teachers at the Stuttgart Waldorf School.

3. For the purpose of gaining an accurate overview of the present membership of the colleges of religion teachers at schools which are members of the Bund, and also for the purpose of making an accurate register of service texts handed out or copied to date, the schools and/or their colleges of religion teachers shall be requested:

a) to supply a list of their religion teachers;
b) to report on which texts (giving the number of the copy or the designation of the copy) are in the possession of which teachers;
c) in respect of every copy of the service texts, to arrange for a declaration in accordance with point 2 to be drawn up and signed, to ensure its safe return to the Stuttgart college of religion teachers;
d) to ascertain which service texts or copies are in the hands of persons who were formerly religion teachers at the respective schools but no longer fulfil any function in connection with the religion lessons or the services; such persons shall be requested to forward any texts or copies they may still have to the Stuttgart college of religion teachers either via their former school or directly.

The texts should be returned personally if possible.

4. The colleges of religion teachers at schools attached to Bund shall meet together at least once a year – most practically on the occasion of a general conference of the Bund in order to consult further about the questions and responsibilities they share.
5. Schools attached to the Bund which are not as yet represented in the general conference of religion teachers are requested – in so far as they have already instituted religion lessons or intend to do so – to accede to this resolution by stating in writing their intention to do so.

Stuttgart, October 16, 1951
(19 signatories on behalf of the college of religion teachers)

Appendix to the 1951 Resolution

> Concerning the appointment of religion teachers at schools belonging to the Bund and concerning the administration of the texts of the 'ritual' services held in conjunction with the religion lessons.

The undersigned representatives of the colleges of religion teachers at schools belonging to the Bund and representatives of the college of religion teachers at the Vrije School, The Hague, further declare their agreement that Dr H. Hahn, as representative of the college of religion teachers at the Stuttgart Waldorf School (Uhlandshöhe) shall undertake the following initiatives:

1. He shall form a small group responsible for the international care of the religion lessons and the services connected with them. Its members should preferably be religion teachers still working in Waldorf schools or Rudolf Steiner schools who were called to this task by Dr Rudolf Steiner himself. This group's task is to encourage responsibility for the religion

lessons and the establishment of protection and good order with regard to these lessons and the services connected with them also in other countries where there are Rudolf Steiner Schools or schools working in the spirit of Waldorf education, in so far as these schools have already established the religion lessons.
2. He shall consult with curative institutions in Germany and elsewhere in so far as the Sunday Services inaugurated by Rudolf Steiner have been established or will be established in them – to bring about suitable regulations befitting the autonomous situation of the curative movement.

Stuttgart, October 16, 1951
(21 signatories on behalf of the college of religion teachers at the Stuttgart Waldorf School)

The Resolution of October 23, 1964

The religion teachers at German Waldorf schools present at the delegates' meeting of October 23, 1964 in Stuttgart resolve the following amendment to the agreement reached on October 16, 1951 regarding the religion lessons and the services connected with them.

A person may be regarded as a religion teacher at a German Waldorf school if he or she has been nominated by the college of religion teachers at the Stuttgart Waldorf School, Uhlandshöhe, and accepted by the Executive Council of the General Anthroposophical Society in Dornach. This resolution is valid forthwith for all newly appointed religion teachers at German Waldorf schools.

Stuttgart, October 23, 1964
(29 signatories).

THE 1983 REVIEW OF THE RESOLUTION OF OCTOBER 1964

by the International Religion Teachers' Gremium

The religion lessons are given by anthroposophists who may be teachers belonging to the college of religion teachers or other persons appointed to do so. Because the religion teachers at the Stuttgart Waldorf School were given a 'ritual' service only a few months after the opening of the school, Rudolf Steiner was particularly concerned that great care should be taken in selecting new religion teachers. The ritual services – the Sunday Service (Class 1 – 8), the Youth Service (Class 8 – 10), the Offering Service (Class 10 upwards to former pupils), and the Christmas Service – form a unity with the religion lessons. The choice of new religion teachers must therefore take into account not only the giving of religion lessons but also the holding of the services.

For the protection of the services and the nomination of new religion teachers, Herbert Hahn, the first religion teacher chosen by Rudolf Steiner, brought into being a gremium comprising religion teachers from the international school movement. Initially the members of this gremium were religion teachers who had been nominated by Rudolf Steiner. We endeavour in this respect to follow Rudolf Steiner's wish, expressed in his farewell letter to the teachers, that through the Internal Council of teachers we should continue to protect his impulses and gifts. The formation of the Gremium and its tasks are described in the Appendix to the 1951 Resolution.

The religion lessons are bound up with the Waldorf School in two ways. Firstly, together with the ritual services and the curriculum developed by Rudolf Steiner before the whole college of teachers in the faculty meetings, they belong to the overall educational plan in which all the subjects mutually carry and fructify one another. Secondly, they 'project' into the [substance of] the school 'like a gulf'. This is an image Rudolf Steiner used to describe the religious instruction in every religious community. He also applied it to the Anthroposophical Society, only in this context anthroposophy is the same spiritual stream out of which the school as a whole with its pedagogy is inaugurated. Thus the religion lessons together with their ritual services are not only bound up with the spiritual source of the school but also with the General Anthroposophical Society and the School of Spiritual Science inaugurated at the Christmas Foundation Meeting. This is given expression in the fact that new religion teachers are reported to Dornach by a member of the Gremium and receive a 'religion teacher's certificate' signed both by the member of the Gremium and by the Executive Council at Dornach.

The ritual texts are given to each school and signed for by one of the teachers responsible for the religion lessons and the services. Each new service holder copies his text from the master copy. The service texts must be kept in a manner befitting personally entrusted esoteric matter.

The texts for the German schools are given out by the Stuttgart Waldorf School (Uhlandshöhe). For other countries, a member of the Gremium responsible for that country carries this out. New religion teachers are selected by the religion teachers at the school in agreement with the full college of teachers and the member of the Gremium. Where a school does not yet have a religion teacher, for example a newly-founded school, that school should consult a member of the Gremium and, where possible, a neighbouring school for advice and assistance in the introduction of the religion lessons within the college of teachers and to the parents.

The room in the school which is prepared for the services must fulfil the necessary conditions. Rudolf Steiner's particulars regarding the altar and the arrangement of the service room form an intrinsic part of the ritual and cannot be arbitrarily changed.

Regarding all questions arising in connection with the establishment of the religion lessons and the services, also in countries where there have hitherto been no or only sporadic religion lessons, we request that contact be made with a member of the Gremium or a member of the Executive Council at the Goetheanum. The associations of Steiner Waldorf schools in the

different countries are also able to give information.
Signed (16 signatories)

The International Religion Teachers' Gremium today

Regional responsibility has become increasingly important as the Steiner Waldorf school movement has expanded. At the 1966 religion teachers' conference in Dornach, therefore, individual members of the Gremium were named together with the country or region for which they were responsible and available for consultation. The names are available from the Pedagogical Section at the Goetheanum in Dornach.

3. The Curriculum and Methods for Different Ages

From Rudolf Steiner's lectures and faculty meetings in chronological order

Faculty Meetings with Rudolf Steiner

Meeting of September 25, 1919

Dr Steiner: We still have to discuss the religion lessons. You should tell the children that whoever wants to have these religion lessons must choose them as such, and then these lessons would simply by a third category beside the other two [Protestant & Catholic]. We absolutely cannot have a muddle. Just go ahead and put those who want the religion lessons together according to their class. You could combine the four lower and the four upper classes. One of us can give the lessons. How many children have opted for these religion lessons?
A teacher: Sixty at the moment, of which 56 are children of anthroposophists. The numbers will still change because some of them want both.
Dr Steiner: As I have already said, we shall not mix the two types of lesson. Neither shall we push these lessons. All we want to do is meet people's wishes. We shall more likely advise the children to attend the denominational lessons. Those children who aren't going to attend any religion lessons at all should not be pressed, but it would not be a bad idea to try and find out why this is. We should find this out in each case. You might get some of them to decide to return to the denominational lessons or to come to the

anthroposophical ones. We should at least do something about those children. We don't want to introduce a situation in which children grow up without any religion lessons at all ...

Dr Steiner: In the lower division everything to do with reincarnation and karma must be excluded. These are not discussed until the children reach the second age group. But then they must be brought in. This should be from the tenth year onwards. With these lessons in particular it is essential to see that the pupils are individually active. Reincarnation and karma must be talked about in a practical way, not theoretically.

As the children approach the age of seven they still have a kind of memory of all kinds of pre-natal conditions. They sometimes describe the oddest things, which are pictorial descriptions of those conditions. An example which is not unusual but typical is when children come and say: I came into the world and it was through a funnel that went on and on. They are describing how they came into the world. Let the children tell you things like this; encourage them in this so that it rises up into consciousness. That is a very good thing to do, only you must avoid putting ideas into their heads. You have to get out of them what they themselves can tell you. This is what you should do. This belongs to the curriculum.

These lessons can be livened up with the sort of thing I spoke about in last night's public lecture.[6] This would be the best thing you could do, basing them simply and solely on an understanding of the human being, without becoming a denominational school. This would perpetually enliven the teaching. The article of mine that will be appearing in the next issue of the *Waldorf Nachrichten* [Waldorf News] also points in this direction. It is on the 'Pedagogical Objective of the Waldorf School'.[7] The indications I give there are essentially a kind of summary for public of all that we have had in the course. I should like you to take what will be in the *Waldorf Nachrichten* as your ideal.

One-and-a-half hours religion per week is sufficient for each group, that is two three-quarter of an hour lessons. It would be especially lovely if they could take place on Sundays, but no doubt

3. THE CURRICULUM AND METHODS FOR DIFFERENT AGES

that would be difficult to arrange. You could also introduce the children to the verses of the *Calendar of the Soul* in these lessons.

A teacher: Aren't they too difficult?

Dr Steiner: We should never do anything that we consider too difficult for the children. It is not a question of taking in the thoughts but how the thoughts follow one another, and so on. I should like to know what could be harder for the children than the Lord's Prayer. It is just that you imagine it to be easier than the verses in the *Calendar of the Soul*. As for the Creed, people object to the Creed only because they do not understand it; if they did, they wouldn't object. It contains only what is obvious, basically, but people do not arrive at an understanding of it by the age of 27, and after that they don't learn any more from life. The discussions about the Creed are childish. There is nothing in it that one could come to a personal decision about. You could also speak the Calendar verses with the children at the beginning of the lesson.

A teacher: Would it be a good thing to let the children speak a kind of morning prayer?

Dr Steiner: This is something that could be done. I had also had it in mind. I will say something about it tomorrow. We will also talk about a prayer. But there is just one thing I should like to ask you. You see, with these things the outer form is of the utmost importance. Never call a verse a 'prayer' but an 'opening verse' for the lesson. Do see to it that people do not hear the teachers calling such a thing a 'prayer'. This will go a long way towards overcoming the prejudice that this is an anthroposophical school.

Meeting of September 26, 1919

A teacher suggested starting the morning with the Lord's Prayer.

Dr Steiner: I should like it very much if you were to begin the lesson with the Lord's Prayer. Then move on to the verses I am going to give you.

For the four lower classes please say the verse as follows:

> The sun with loving light
> Makes bright for me each day,
> The soul with spirit power
> Gives strength into my limbs.
> In sunlight shining clear
> I reverence, O God,
> The strength of human kind
> Which Thou so graciously
> Hast planted in my soul,
> That I, with all my might
> May love to work and learn.
> From Thee comes light and strength,
> To Thee rise love and thanks.

The pupils should feel it in the way I spoke it. They will have to take in the words first, and then you would gradually have to bring home to them the contrast between what is outside and what is inside.

> The sun with loving light
> Makes bright for me each day,
> The soul with spirit power
> Gives strength into my limbs.

The first part is what you notice by means of observation: the light making the day bright. The second part refers to the soul feeling in the limbs. Soul and spirit – physical and bodily: that is what this passage contains.

> In sunlight shining clear
> I reverence, O God,
> The strength of human kind
> Which Thou so graciously
> Hast planted in my soul,
> That I, with all my might
> May love to work and learn.

3. THE CURRICULUM AND METHODS FOR DIFFERENT AGES

This is directed, reverently, to the same two aspects. Then, turning to each once more:

> From Thee comes light and strength (*the sun*)
> To Thee rise love and thanks. (*from within*)

That is how I think the children should feel it: as speaking to the divine that is both in the light and in the soul.

You must try and speak it with the children in chorus with the feeling with which I have read it to you. First of all the children will just learn the words, until they know words, beat and rhythm. Later on, when an occasion offers, you can say. 'Let's have a look and see what it is about.' They must know it first before you explain it. Don't explain it first, or attach too much importance to the children knowing it by heart. They should learn it by heart gradually, through speaking it repeatedly. Initially they should just read it from your lips. If it goes badly for a long time, say four weeks, it will go all the better later on. The older ones can write it down, but you have to teach it to the youngest ones gradually. Don't tell them they have to learn it by heart! It would be nice if you were to write it down for them; then they would have it in your handwriting.

...

Therefore we shall have two levels. We will take the children of the four lower classes together, and then make another group of those from the four upper classes.

In the four lower classes we will endeavour to discuss with the children things and processes in our human surroundings in such a way that there arises in them the feeling that there is spirit in nature. The kind of things that will come into consideration will be like those in the examples I gave. Let us say you want to teach the children the concept of soul. First of all it will be absolutely necessary to teach them the concept of life. You can bring this concept of life to the understanding of the children by drawing their attention to the fact that to begin with human beings are small, then they grow up, and eventually they get old, with white hair, wrinkles, etc. In drawing their attention to the seriousness of the human biography you also acquaint them with the earnestness of death, for they are bound to encounter this too.

It is also valuable to make a comparison between what goes on in the human soul in the interchange between sleeping and waking. You can perfectly well go into these things with even the youngest children in the lower group. Waking and sleeping: discuss the phenomenon of the soul being at rest and the human being's immobility while asleep, and so on. Then talk with the children about the soul coming into the body when they wake up, and make them aware that they have a will that is active in their limbs; draw their attention to the fact that the body gives the soul its senses through which they see, hear and so on. Things like this are a proof that spirit holds sway in the physical. All this can be discussed with the children.

You must completely avoid teaching them any superficial theory about expediency. Anthroposophical religion lessons must on no account tend towards offering a theory of expediency after the manner of the following example, 'Why do we find cork on trees?' 'So that we can make stoppers for champagne bottles. God in His wisdom arranged it like that, so that we have cork for stoppers.' This business of things being there for a reason, and working in nature in the same way as human purpose, is deadly; this must not be cultivated. On no account use superficial notions of expediency to explain nature.

Nor must we cultivate the idea, of which people are so fond, that the Unknown is a proof of the spirit. People say, don't they, 'Oh, we cannot know that, spirit is being revealed there!' Instead of people having the feeling that they can know about the spirit, and that spirit is indeed revealed in matter, they are very drawn to the idea that when they cannot explain something it is because it is a proof of the divine.

So these two things must be strictly avoided: a superficial expediency theory, and seeking out the miraculous as an explanation of divine purpose.

On the contrary, it is very important that we develop the kind of ideas with which we can point from nature to the supersensible. For instance I have often given this particular example: we can speak to the children about the chrysalis of the butterfly, telling them about the butterfly coming out of the chrysalis, and we can convey the concept of the immortal soul in this connection if we tell them how when human beings die their soul comes forth like an invisible butterfly, just as the butterfly comes out of the chrysalis. However, this sort of idea has an effect only if you yourself believe in it, only if this idea of the butterfly coming out of the chrysalis is also for you a symbol of eternity placed in nature by divine powers. You have to believe in it yourself, otherwise the children will not believe you.

You must encourage things like this in the children. They will work particularly strongly in the children if you can give them examples of how a creature can live in many forms; one primary form in many different forms. The important thing in the religion lessons is to foster a *feeling* for these things rather than develop a world conception. For instance you can use the poems about the metamorphosis of the plants and the animals quite well from a religious point of view; you just have to make sure that you make use of the feelings that flow from line to line. You can look at nature in a similar way up to the end of Class 4. In particular you should keep on encouraging the thought that in all his thinking and action the human being stands within the whole cosmos. You must also encourage the thought that God is there in what lives within us. You must return again and again to thoughts such as these: God is in the leaves of the trees and in the sun; God is in the clouds and in the stream. God is also flowing in our blood and living in our heart and in everything we feel and everything we think. Develop the idea wherever you can that the human being, too, is steeped in the divine.

Already at this early age you must encourage the idea very strongly that because man is an image of God and a revelation of the divine it is his duty to be good. Human beings harm God if they are not good. From the religious point of view human beings are not in this world for their own sake but in order to be a revelation of God. People often express this by saying that the human being is not here for his own sake but for the 'glory of God'. 'Glory' here means 'revelation,' just as 'glory to God in the highest' really means 'the gods are being revealed in the heights.' Thus the expression that man exists 'to the Glory of god' is to be understood as meaning that he exists in order to express the divine in his whole feeling and actions. Thus if he does something bad or lacks piety and kindness, he is a disgrace before God, disfigures Him and makes Him ugly.

You must make a special point of this idea. God dwelling in man is a conception that should be made use of even at this youngest stage. I would keep away from any kind of Christology at this stage and awaken a feeling of the divine Father solely of nature and natural processes. I should also try to combine this with all kinds of discussion on motifs in the Old Testament, in so far as they are suitable – and they are suitable if handled properly – the Psalms of David, the Song of Solomon, etc. That, then, is the first stage.

At the second stage, which would comprise the four upper classes, you should spend a lot of time discussing the concepts of destiny, the destiny of individuals. The children must learn what destiny is, so that they really feel that the human being has a destiny. It is important that the children learn the difference between what happens accidentally and what is destiny. So you have to deal with the subject of destiny with the children. The question about whether something that happens to you is destiny or chance cannot be answered by a definition. But it can perhaps be answered by means of examples. What I mean is that if I feel that something that happens to me is happening through my own choice, then it is destiny. If I cannot feel that I chose it but feel very strongly that it has taken me by surprise and that I can learn a lot from it for the future, then it is chance and will become future destiny. It is through this kind of thing, which is a matter of feeling, that the children gradually have to be taught the difference between 'karma accomplished' and 'karma in the making'. You really should take the children by degrees through the question of destiny in the sense of karma.

3. THE CURRICULUM AND METHODS FOR DIFFERENT AGES

That there are different kinds of feeling you will find explained in greater detail in the latest edition of my book *Theosophy*. I have dealt with this problem in the chapter on reincarnation and karma, which I have completely revised. I have tried to develop the theme of how one can sense the difference. You can certainly draw the children's attention to the fact that there are actually two kinds of events. With the first kind you have a feeling that you chose it. For instance, when you get to know someone you usually feel that you have sought him out. But if you are involved in a natural event you feel you can learn a lot from it for the future. If something happens to you that is caused by other people, it is usually fulfilled karma. Even meeting together like this, for instance, in a college of teachers in the Waldorf School, is fulfilled karma. You get together like this because you have sought one another. You cannot define this in thought, however, but only feel it. You must talk to the children about all kinds of particular destinies that demonstrate the problem of destiny, perhaps in story form. You can even repeat some things from fairy tales and take those stories through again that contain questions of destiny. But the best place to find examples of this is in history, where you see destiny being fulfilled in the lives of individual people. The matter of destiny is the thing that has to be discussed now, in order to show the serious reality of life from this point of view.

I should now like to speak to you about what religion really is from an anthroposophical point of view. Religion in the anthroposophical sense is feeling, the kind of feeling our world conception awakens in us for the world, for the spirit, and for life. The world conception itself is a matter for the head, but the religious element always arises out of the whole human being. That is why a denominational religion is not really religious. The important thing is that the whole human being, especially his feeling and will, is involved in religion. The world conception part of religion is really only there for exemplification, to support and deepen the feeling and to strengthen the will. What should result from religion is that the human being grows beyond what transitory, earthly things can contribute to his life of feeling and will.

You would have to go on from the question of destiny to discuss the difference between what is inherited from parents and what is brought by the human being from an earlier incarnation. With the older group earlier lives on earth are referred to, and you do all you can to help the children both understand and feel that the human being passes through repeated lives on earth.

Then you ought by all means to enlarge on the fact that the human being, as he is now, attains to divinity in three stages. That is, after you have taken your time over teaching the children, through stories, the concepts of heredity and repeated earth lives alongside the concept of destiny, you go on to the three stages of the divine.

The first level of divinity leads to the angel who exists personally for each individual human being. You discuss how each individual person is led from one life to another by his guardian angel. This is what you discuss first, this personal divinity that guides the human being.

Secondly you endeavour to explain to the children the existence of higher gods, the Archangels, who direct whole groups of people, nations and suchlike. Little by little you approach aspects that can lead over into history and geography. This has to be so clearly contrasted that the children learn to distinguish between the god who is spoken of in Protestantism, for instance, who is really only an angel, and an archangel, who is a higher being than anything occurring in the Protestant religious teachings.

Thirdly you have to teach them the idea of a Time Spirit as a divine being ruling over whole periods of time. Here you approach the connection between history and religion.

Not until you have taught concepts like these can you go further, around the twelfth year – but we cannot do this yet. We shall have two groups, and it will be alright for the children to hear sooner what they will understand better later on. After we have taught the children as much as possible about the three stages, we proceed to Christology proper, by dividing world evolution into two parts: the pre-Christian era, which is a preparation, then the Christian era, which is a fulfilment. You must lay great emphasis

3. THE CURRICULUM AND METHODS FOR DIFFERENT AGES

on the concept of the divine revealing itself through Christ 'in the fullness of time'.

After this, but not before, you can go on to the gospels. Prior to this you can turn to the Old Testament for the stories you need to illustrate the concept of angels, archangels and the Time Spirit. For instance, you can take the appearance of Moses from the Old Testament to show the beginning of a new spirit of the age, compared with the earlier age when Moses had not yet given his revelations. Then you show that a new Time Spirit arose in the sixth century BC. You show this first of all in the Old Testament. Eventually, when you have passed on to Christology and shown what a long time went into its preparation, you start on the gospels and try taking out parts of them, showing the children what a natural thing it is to have four aspects in the four gospels. Just as a tree has to be photographed from four sides to be seen properly, the gospels are like four points of view. Take something from the Gospel of Matthew, from the Gospel of Mark, from the Gospel of Luke, from the Gospel of John, and make sure that the feeling content strikes home. Put the chief emphasis on the different feelings the various gospels call forth.

That then is the syllabus for the older group. The main feature for the younger group is that everything you bring the growing child shall be evidence of the wisdom of God in nature.

For the older group you have transformation: the human being does not know God through wisdom alone, but through the active working of love.

That is the leitmotif for the two groups.

A teacher: Should we let the children learn verses?

Dr Steiner: Yes, chiefly from the Old Testament, and later on from the New Testament. Not the verses that are often found in prayer books, as they are usually too trite. So take verses from the Bible and also from what we have in the way of anthroposophical verses. We have a wide choice that can easily be used in the anthroposophical religion lessons.

A teacher: Should we teach the ten commandments?

Dr Steiner: The ten commandments are in the Old Testament, of course, but the children would have to be made aware of how seriously they should be taken. It says there that the name of God should not be spoken in vain, which is something I keep stressing. Nearly every speaker from the pulpit violates this, by perpetually uttering the name of Christ in vain. Such things must be made clear at the feeling level, of course. The religion lessons must altogether be given with depth of feeling instead of in a denominational form. The Creed itself is not as important as the feeling it engenders. Faith in the Father, Son and Holy Spirit is not what matters most, but rather how people feel towards them, so that in the depths of our soul we are aware that:

◊ Not to acknowledge God is an illness;
◊ Not to acknowledge Christ is destiny, a misfortune;
◊ Not to acknowledge the Holy Spirit is a narrow-mindedness of the human soul.

A teacher: Should we give the children the historical facts such as those appertaining to the progress of the Zarathustra individuality up to the revelation of Christianity, or the story of the two Jesus boys?
Dr Steiner: You must round off the religion lessons by bringing these connections to the children, but with great discretion of course. For the younger group you have more a religion of nature, for the older ones more an historical religion.

Meeting of December 23, 1919

Two teachers report on the religion lessons.
Dr Steiner: You could try in the religion lessons to develop imaginative things such as the mythical religious symbols, for instance the Mithras symbol as the conquest of the lower nature. You could use religious symbols like this in order to emphasise the pictorial element, and develop the narrative round these.
There is a question about reports.
Dr Steiner: You would have to find out what is prescribed. We could give two reports, one in the middle of the year as an interim

report, and another at the end of the school year. As far as the powers-that-be permit it, just write general information about the pupils in these reports. Characterise the pupil, and only mention a particular subject if it is specifically outstanding. Be as positive as you can, and as the pupils move up into the higher classes do not grade them more than is absolutely necessary.

If they move on to another school you must give a report on the sort of things the next school requires to know.

The Renewal of Education

Basle, May 7, 1920

It is of great importance for a living comprehension of history to look upon outer events as symptoms of hidden causes which one begins to divine more and more, if one continues to observe them with an open and searching mind. If one looks at history in this way, one will also gradually discover ascending lines of development, culminating in certain events, and followed by periods of decline. And this is where we come face to face with the event of Golgotha. If we can recognise in outer happenings evidence of inner processes, we will find ourselves gradually moving into a religious sphere. Then history will become permeated by a religious element. This will open the way towards a new understanding of a subject which pupils had been given already at a younger age, namely of the gospels, or the Old Testament. Previously it was not yet possible to convey a deeper meaning of this subject, neither was it necessary then. First it was introduced in narrative form but later, when pupils are ready for a more mature conception of history, the contents of the Bible will also live anew. It is a good thing for this subject to reach a climax by degrees, and this is made possible through an approach to history that looks at symptoms because, through it, the religious impulse and experience are deepened.

Faculty Meetings with Rudolf Steiner

Meeting of June 14, 1920

A teacher reports on the religion lessons in the lower and the second group. There has been a discussion about verses from the Mystery Plays and Angelus Silesius' Cherubinischer Wandersmann.

Dr Steiner: The important thing is to bear in mind whether the children's feeling life is sufficiently mature. Can you give me a concrete example?

A teacher: With the top group I have been reciting *'Lass mich ruhend in dir wirken'*.

Dr Steiner: Did you find that the children could make anything of it? Yes? Then you can persevere with it.

A teacher: Perhaps we could divide the groups.

Dr Steiner: Yes, that is certainly possible. If the lower group were to be divided into two, and the top group stays the same, there would be three groups, that is Classes 1–3, Classes 4–6, and Classes 7–9.

A teacher reports on the preparation lesson for the Youth Service saying he has taken three hours over it.

Dr Steiner: Isn't that overburdening the pupils? How many are there?

A teacher: Twenty-six.

Dr Steiner: It will be difficult to say anything about it until we have made a real success of it. It is a good thing to give it a try. If it does not work we shall have to see how else we could do it.

A teacher reports on his social studies lessons. He had had two lessons a week with Classes 6–8 and a few children from Class 5.

Dr Steiner: Of course that is a difficult age, the eleventh to the fifteenth year, but it is a lesson apart.

A teacher: We also visit factories.

Dr Steiner: If you do it in a really living way and connect it with life in all kinds of ways just at this age, then it will be all right. I should try to see that the children do not get too much of it; and connect it with life as much as possible.

3. THE CURRICULUM AND METHODS FOR DIFFERENT AGES

I believe too much demand is made on the children's time. The overstrain is sure to make itself felt somewhere. It would be a good thing to avoid having eight lessons in one day.

I cannot see why you need three hours to prepare for the Youth Service. Why shouldn't one hour be enough? It is not the amount that is important but the period of time during which the whole thing is carried out. These things can certainly be curtailed, and perhaps it would be better if they were. What you could do would be to let those preparing for the Youth Service miss the religion lesson and use that time for preparing for the Youth Service.

Meeting of September 22, 1920

Dr Steiner: In the religion lessons with this group of Classes 7, 8 and 9 we can now move on to giving them a theoretical explanation, in a free way, of things like pre-existence and life after death, all that results from pre-existence. Give them examples. Present them with the broad cultural connections, showing them how to look at this. The mission of human beings on the earth. You need only look at Goethe or Jean Paul from this point of view, and you can see and demonstrate at every point that their capacities stem from pre-earthly life.

Then there is a very good picture that can really be raised into the religious sphere, and that is the figure of Laocoön. What is really happening in the statue is that the etheric body is separating from the physical, hence the distortions of the latter. You can demonstrate a great deal in connection with the breaking up of the physical body of Laocoön. You ought to have a picture of the group. But this awe in the presence of the disintegrating physical body must be raised on to the religious level.

Meeting of May 26, 1921

Dr Steiner: We must awaken in the children a feeling for the seasons of the year. And we must pay more attention to giving the children as living a picture of the Christ as we can, making that the focal point, at all the stages, so that we come back to it again and again and let the whole of Christ's earthly life be at the centre. A personal relationship with the Christ must be cherished, even in the lower classes, so that it arises like a kind of inner ritual. Cherish the children's personal relationship with Christ! There must be a real religious mood in the lessons. Symbols and images must play their part so that the children's feelings are very strongly engaged.

Education for Adolescents

Stuttgart, June 13, 1921

There are spiritual connections in life. If we have first heard a song in our mind, in the spirit, it will have a greater effect on the children when we teach it to them. These things are related. The spiritual world works in the physical. This activity, this work of the spiritual world, must be applied especially to education and didactics. If, for example, during the preparation for a religion lesson, the teacher experiences a naturally pious mood, the lesson will have a profound effect on the children. When such a mood is absent, the lesson will be of little value to them.

Stuttgart, June 15, 1921

Let us consider an extreme case. Let us think of a prayer. The children should, when asked to learn a prayer, be urged to be in a mood of devotion. It is up to us to see to this. We must almost feel a horror if we teach the children without first establishing this mood of reverence or devotion. And they should never say a prayer without this mood. We should also not make the children recite a lovely poem without first arousing in them a faint smile, a pleasure or joy; we should not order them to have these feelings but rather allow the content of the poem to awaken them. This principle applies to other subjects as well.

3. THE CURRICULUM AND METHODS FOR DIFFERENT AGES

Stuttgart, June 15, 1921

It is most important during puberty that the children have developed certain moral, religious feelings. Such feelings also strengthen the astral body and ego. They become weak if the religious, moral feelings and impulses have been neglected. The children then turn indolent, as though physically paralyzed. This will show itself especially during the years we are not discussing. The lack of moral and ethical impulses also leads to irregularities in the sexual life.

We must consider the differences between girls and boys in our education leading up to this age. We must make the effort to develop the girls' moral and ethical feelings in a way that they are directed toward the aesthetic life. We must take special care that the girls especially enjoy the moral, the religious, and the good in what they hear in the lessons. They should take pleasure in the knowledge that the world is permeated by the supersensible; they should be given pictures that are rich in imagination, that express the world as permeated by the divine, that show the beautiful aspects of the good and moral human being.

In regard to boys, it will be necessary to provide them with ideas and mental pictures that tend toward strength and affect the religious and ethical life. With girls, we should bring the religious and moral life to their very eyes, while with boys we should bring the religious and beautiful predominantly into the heart, the mind, stressing the feeling of strength that radiates from them. Naturally, we must not take these things to an extreme, should not think of making the girls into aesthetic kittens that regard everything merely aesthetically. Nor should the boys be made into mere louts, as would be the inevitable result of their egotisms being engendered through the unduly strong feeling of their strength – which we ought to awaken, but only by connecting it to the good, the beautiful, and the religious.

We must prevent the girls from becoming superficial, from becoming unhealthy, sentimental connoisseurs of beauty during their teenage years. And we must prevent the boys from turning into hooligans. These dangers exist. We must know the reality of these tendencies and must, during the whole of elementary education, see to it that the girls are directed to experience pleasure in the beautiful, to be impressed by the religious and aesthetic aspects of the lessons; and we must see to it that the boys are told, 'If you do this, your muscles will grow taut, you will become a strong, efficient young man!' The sense of being permeated by the divine must really be kindled in boys in this way.

Faculty Meetings with Rudolf Steiner

Meeting of June 17, 1921

Dr Steiner: In the religion lessons we haven't got as far as doing psalms with the children yet. It would be the ten-year-olds who should understand the psalms. Discuss the whole subject matter contained in a psalm; make a kind of inward study of what it contains, and then you can crown it all by singing it.

A teacher: What shall I take next? I'm coming to an end with tales.

Dr Steiner: Symbolism connected with suitable themes. The significance of the festivals of the year. There is so much material in the lectures on the Christmas, Easter and Whitsun festivals. You can discuss most of what is in those lectures. If you bring it forward in the right way it will be good for this age group in particular. Link up with the relevant festivals as closely as possible, but you can begin before the festival and continue beyond it. Work at the Christmas festival for four weeks.

A teacher: When I take the prophets, can I use Michelangelo's figures?

Dr Steiner: Yes, that would be alright.

A teacher: Should we derive anything from the realm of sculpture?

Dr Steiner: It would be good to know how far you have taken this and how you yourself would have continued.

Pass on to studying the psalms. Then take the Laocoön group, so that we can dwell on the elements of tragedy and the sublime.

The Laocoön group is the moment of death.

A teacher: May I continue in this way in the religion lessons for Classes 3 and 4?

Dr Steiner: Don't imagine that you can leave the Christ out. You must not do that.

A teacher: I was doing the history of the Old Testament.

Dr Steiner: Not exclusively Old Testament history.

A teacher: What shall I begin with in Class 1?

Dr Steiner: On the whole we have always tried to begin by reflecting on the phenomena of nature. This was one of the themes even for the youngest group. Then we gradually moved on to stories that have been made up. Then we came to the gospels and worked on scenes from the Gospel of John. Our starting point was a kind of nature religion. It is a matter of leading the children in a natural way to the experience of religious feelings, by drawing their attention to all kinds of things.

Regarding the lessons of a religion teacher who could not hold the attention of the children, so that they were walking about in the classroom.

Dr Steiner: That sort of thing must never happen a second time. It is a colossal failure. It mustn't be like it was in Haubinda.* Some of the children lay on the floor and stuck their legs in the air, while others lounged on the window sill and the desks. Not one sat properly on a chair. A story by Keller was being read to them. There was no religious atmosphere at all. That was in 1903.

Waldorf Education and Anthroposophy, Vol. 1

Kristiania (Oslo), November 23, 1921

During the ninth and tenth year, however, another feeling also lives in the child, often only dimly and vaguely felt. This is the

---

* When lecturing nearby Steiner visited the newly-founded Hermann Lietz boarding school in Haubinda.

feeling that those who are the objects of such authority must themselves also look up to something higher. A natural outcome of this direct, tangible relationship between the teacher and the child is the child's awareness of the teacher's own religious feelings and of the way in which the teacher relates to the metaphysical world- all. Such imponderables must not be overlooked in teaching and education. People of materialistic outlook usually believe that whatever affects children reaches them only through words or outer actions. Little do they know that quite other forces are at work in children.

Let us consider something which occasionally happens. Let us assume that a teacher thinks, 'I – as teacher – am an intelligent person, but my pupils are very ignorant. If I want to communicate a feeling for the immortality of the human soul to my students, I can think, for instance, of what happens when a butterfly emerges from a chrysalis. I can compare this event, this picture, with what happens when a person dies. Thus I can say to my children, "Just as the butterfly flies out of the chrysalis, so, after death, the immortal soul leaves the physical body." Such a comparison, I am certain, offers a useful simile for the child's benefit.'

But if the picture – the simile – is chosen with an attitude of mental superiority on the part of the teacher, we find that it does not touch the pupils at all and, soon after hearing it, they forget all about it, because the teacher did not believe in the truth of his simile.

Anthroposophy teaches us to believe in such a picture and I can assure you that, for me, the butterfly emerging from the chrysalis is not a simile that I have invented. For me, the butterfly emerging out of the chrysalis is a revelation on a lower plane of what on a higher level represents the immortality of the human soul. As far as I am concerned, it is not I who created this picture out of my own reasoning; rather, it is the world itself that reveals the process of nature in the emergence of a butterfly. That is what this picture means to me. I believe with every fibre of my soul that it represents a truth placed by the gods themselves before our eyes. I do not imagine that, compared with the child, I am wiser and the child more foolish. I believe in the truth of this picture with the same earnestness that I wish to awaken in the child. If a teacher teaches with such an attitude, the child will remember it for the rest of his or her life.

Unseen supersensible – or shall we say imponderable – forces are at work here. It is not the words that we speak to children that matter, but what we ourselves are – and above all what we are when we are dealing with our children. This is especially important during the period between the ninth and tenth years, for it is during this time that the child feels the underlying background out of which a teacher's words are spoken. Goethe said, 'Consider well the *what*, but consider more the *how*.' A child can see whether an adult's words express a genuine relationship with the supersensible world or whether they are spoken with a materialistic attitude – the words have a different 'ring'. The child experiences a difference of quality between the two approaches. During this period between the ninth and tenth years, children need to feel, if only subconsciously, that as they look up to the authority of their teachers, their teacher likewise looks up to what no longer is outwardly visible. Then, through the relationship of teacher to child, a feeling for other people becomes transformed into a religious experience.

Soul Economy

Dornach, December 30, 1921

And so the teacher, having duly prepared himself in the way just indicated, enters the school building in the morning. The pupils arrive at school a little earlier in summer-time (at eight o'clock), and a little later during the winter. When they are assembled in their classrooms, the teacher brings them together by speaking a morning verse in chorus with the whole class. This verse, which could also be sung and which embraces both a general human as well as a religious element, unites the pupils in a mood of prayer. It can be followed by a genuine prayer. In our Independent

Waldorf School such details are entirely left to the discretion of each individual teacher.

Faculty Meetings with Rudolf Steiner

Meeting of January 14, 1922

A teacher: In Class 3 the stories should be from the Bible. I don't know how to do this.

Dr Steiner: Get one of the older Catholic editions of the Bible. That will show you how to retell these stories. They are done quite well, only you must do better still. That will give you the chance to avoid Luther's frightful translation. Altogether it would be a good thing to take the Catholic translation. Also I would recommend you to study the pre-Lutheran translations, so that you can learn to see through the myth about Luther's tremendous merit in having translated the Bible. We are badly haunted by the idea that Luther did a great service to the formation of the German language. It is something that is really ingrained in the minds of Central Europeans. If you go back to earlier translations and look at longer passages you will see what splendid work was done compared with Luther's translation, which has actually stunted the evolution of the German language to a dreadful extent.

There is an edition of the Bible for children, the Schuster Bible.[8] You can always get hold of it in a region where there are a good many Catholics. Begin before the Creation, with the fall of the angels. The Catholic Bible begins with the fall of the angels, and the Creation comes after that. It is very nice; a simple, straightforward narrative.

Meeting of May 10, 1922

Dr Steiner: I should like to discuss a few important points.
A teacher: What should we take in art in Class 11?
Dr Steiner: One possibility would certainly be to take art in its

connection with the whole of cultural development; they might show a good understanding of this. Call their attention to the question of why music in its present form arose relatively late. What did the ancient Greeks call music? This sort of thing. Then it would naturally follow, wouldn't it, that you discuss in detail the kind of things that were touched on in the German lesson today from the aspect of literature. Why did landscape painting begin at a specific time? Especially this kind of question. Then art and religion, from the artistic point of view.

A religion teacher asks a question on this subject.

Dr Steiner: Religion lessons ought to strike a different note. In the history of art everything should be directed towards an understanding of the artistic element. In the religion lessons I should have thought we ought to aim at creating a religious mood. It should be a kind of religious upbringing. Formerly a strong emphasis was laid on the intellectual element in religion.

Meeting of June 21, 1922

Dr Steiner: Class 11 religion lessons. It will lead to discussion if you take it in a way that calls on their power of judgment. The important thing previously was pictorial representation. Now the time has come when you really should try to work towards concepts. Deal with questions of destiny in a religious way; guilt and atonement; Father, Son, Spirit. You work from pictures towards concepts, which will be a kind of study in cause and effect.

What have they definitely had in religion in Classes 8 and 9?

A teacher: We set out from a study of the Laocoön group.

Dr Steiner: It is not necessary to go through all of it. I imagine you have taken parts of the Gospel of John. It is very difficult to take the story of the Creation with children unless you have made a close study of it. You do not need any other chapter of the Old Testament. I should think it would be a good idea if you were to take the Acts of the Apostles with the children who know the New Testament. You can do it in connection with the Gospel of Luke.

RELIGIOUS EDUCATION IN STEINER-WALDORF SCHOOLS

Meeting of June 22, 1922

Dr Steiner: I should like you to bring forward all the questions you feel to be urgent. But I just wanted to say one thing. In the religion lessons it is essential you continue with everything you have been doing up to now. But it is also necessary that from the lowest class upwards the children are brought into a mood of prayer in their lessons. By degrees you must create a very strong mood of prayer. The children must get to know the mood of prayer. You must convey, 'not my will but Thine be done.' They must rise to the level where the divine is at work. In the religion lessons you must not only use pictures but the children must be directed towards that uplifted mood. You must instil in them a mood which links up with the Sunday Service, and get them to feel the mood of prayer there.

Erziehung zum Leben

The Hague, November 4, 1922 (Trans. J.C.)

In this public lecture Rudolf Steiner describes the seven-year periods with particular reference to religious education and the development of the child.

Let me once again use an example to illustrate what I mean. Suppose the teacher is to instruct the child about the immortality of the human soul in a simple form suitable for children. This has to be done by means of a picture, for between the change of teeth and puberty children are chiefly adjusted to receiving pictures rather than abstract concepts. They also still accept things on the basis of their teacher's unquestioned authority.

There are two ways of bringing this picture to the children. You can say, 'I, the teacher, am tremendously clever while the children are still quite stupid. I am to instruct them with regard to the immortality of the soul, and I shall do this by means of a

3. THE CURRICULUM AND METHODS FOR DIFFERENT AGES

picture. I shall use the picture of the chrysalis out of which the butterfly creeps, to show how the soul extricates itself from the physical body in death, as though out of a chrysalis, and flies away into the spiritual world.'

I am not saying that this is a philosophical proof, which it certainly is not. But it is a way of giving the children an image. And, as I have said, you can use it in the manner just described, claiming as a teacher to know all about such things through being clever while the children are stupid, and deciding to teach this image to the children. Foolish though it may be, you expect the children to believe in it.

Well, dear friends, you will achieve nothing if you approach the children in this manner. Although they may memorize what you tell them, you will not achieve what you should set out to achieve, which is to raise their level of soul experience, and to fill their soul with strong and living content. You can achieve this if you set about it in a different way, not by saying, 'As the teacher I am clever while the children are stupid,' but by saying to yourself (if you will forgive me for speaking in paradoxes), 'Perhaps these children are far cleverer than I am in the unconscious depths of their soul, perhaps I am the stupid one.' This is indeed true in some ways. Those who know how the as yet unformed inner organs, especially the brain, will be formed by the still unconscious, dreaming soul of the child, and how tremendous wisdom works on this especially in the earliest years of childhood, those who are able to appreciate such things, those who are not philistines lacking in appreciation of such things, will say to themselves, 'All the wisdom we attain during our life, however marvellous the machines it manages to construct, is not as far advanced as the unconscious wisdom of a child.'

A teacher whose way of teaching is founded on anthroposophy will himself believe in the comparison of the butterfly emerging from its chrysalis. Such a teacher knows that this comparison is not his invention, for it is put there by nature itself. What on a higher level is the emergence of the immortal soul from the body, this has been given a precursor by nature in the butterfly emerging from its chrysalis. By imbuing with our own feelings the image we present to the children we are giving them something right and proper, for by doing this we are giving them strength for life. Nothing will work on the children in the right way unless we believe in it ourselves with all our strength. These are the imponderable factors at work between teacher and pupil, something that cannot be expressed in words but lies only in an exchange of feelings; this is the supersensible work in our teaching. If it is absent, then only the grosser factors are at work, not the imponderables, so that what we pass on to the children is not what they will really need on their path through life.

By saying these things I wanted to point out how the artistic element, indeed a pious mood in our approach to the being of the child, is something that belongs in our education and the way we teach. This is especially obvious with regard to the religious and moral education we want to give the children.

...

A child who has been surrounded by gratitude and love will finally also learn that a human being is not complete unless he regards himself as the one who carries out the divine world order, the good in the world in earthly existence. When moral education is founded on gratitude, so that egoism is overcome in a healthy way – not by means of mystic, moralistic lecturing or by sentimentality – when gratitude has been transformed into love in a healthy and not in a sentimental way, then one will be able to lead the young people who love the world towards knowing that the human being in body, soul and spirit is just as much a spiritual cripple if he does not become a bearer of the good as is someone who is crippled through having lost a leg. In imagination, in etheric spiritual knowledge, we learn to recognize that it is the good that makes the human being properly complete. Just as when you glance at a drawing of the nervous system or the blood system and see it as a shadow picture of the human being, so do you see in imaginative knowledge how the good is an image of the complete human being.

This is where moral and religious education combine. This

is where it becomes meaningful to say that God is the source of all good, and that the human being is the image, the likeness of God. Religious and moral education are united in this. Through moral, religious education we must ensure that human beings feel and take this feeling into their will, for only as moral beings are they true human beings, whereas if they do not desire what is moral they are not entirely complete. When we learn to educate human beings in such a way that they honestly feel robbed of their humanity if they do not become good, moral people, then shall we have given them a proper religious and a proper moral education.

Do not say that it is all too easy to talk of such things but that they can only remain in the realm of ideals because in the ordinary world nothing can ever be perfect. Of course the ordinary world cannot be perfect, as those of us who speak out of spiritual science know quite confidently and accurately. Nevertheless, the mood we can imbue ourselves with in our teaching, the way our enthusiasm can lead us to be fully understood by the feelings of the child's soul, so that we can find a path to his will, this is contained in what I have just said; it is contained in a true understanding of the human being that culminates in the sentence: only the morally good human being is a complete human being, and the morally good human being is imbued with religious impulses.

Thus must we lead all education to a culmination in moral, religious education. We must also know that the human being bears within him a time organism, and that we must learn to observe this time organism through spiritual knowledge of the human being in every hour, every week, every year during which it is our task to teach the child, going lovingly into every detail.

Faculty Meetings with Rudolf Steiner

Meeting of December 9, 1922

There is a question about Wolfram von Eschenbach's Parzival *in Class 11.*
Dr Steiner: Of course both in the religion lessons and in history lessons the essential aspect is how to deal with it. The crux of the matter is how to deal with it in the two different spheres. In the religion lessons you will have to lay the main emphasis on bringing out the differences between the three stages in Parzival's life. First, his comparative state of innocence while he lived the life of a simpleton. Secondly, his state of heart torment: 'If doubt is born in the heart, that must be sour for the soul.' And thirdly, the inner assurance and certainty of what he has achieved, what is connected with the 'wholeness of soul'.

This aspect will be especially developed in the religion lessons, the whole story being told with this in view, and you would also show them that at the time when Wolfram wrote *Parzival* there was the religious conviction prevailing in certain classes of the population that every human being has these three stages in his own life of soul; that this was considered the right way to think about the progressive development of the human soul. You can speak of the parallelism between the almost simultaneous appearance of Wolfram's legend and Dante's [*Divine Comedy*], although Dante's is quite different. If you go into it you should give the different stages a religious colouring.

In the literature and history lessons you would show the youngsters how it emerges from an earlier stage and runs on into a later one. That up to the ninth or tenth century the laity rightly obeyed the enlightened priesthood in a totally simple-minded way. And that the Parzival problem then made its appearance because the laity itself began to want to have a say in what they received from the priesthood. That Wolfram von Eschenbach himself was actually in a similar situation to that of the young Parzival, and of ordinary lay people, with regard to the priesthood. Wolfram still could not write [he dictated his book], but in his inner life he took a keen part in what was going on.

Historically Wolfram is an interesting phenomenon which shows up this whole time of transition. He cannot write, the laity have not yet acquired access to education, but the corresponding soul experiences were already well in evidence. Therefore it is of historical significance that the clergyman, the cleric, is the writer, the one who can write. We still find it in *Faust* right up to the sixteenth century: 'I'm cleverer, true, than those fops of teachers, doctors and magisters, scribes and preachers.' The scribes are the clerics, the ones in control of the instruments of external culture. This only changes when printing comes into existence. The culture of Parzival's time was the culture preceding that of the printing press.

You must try to enter the language element. Dwell on the fact that you can clearly see in *Parzival* that expressions like 'simpleton', which includes the aspects of both mental twilight and ignorance, were an expressive description of how people felt in those times. By the time Goethe came along being 'simple' was a kind of affectation. He addressed the dog's tail-wagging as though it were the personification of doubt, which in *Faust* for instance just means that he wags his tail. This fact of doubt having a connection with going in two directions, and that a dog's tail moves to the left and right, dividing the dog in half, was no longer felt at all in later times. The soul element became completely abstract, whereas Goethe felt it to be the ultimate stage of concrete reality. The fact that Goethe took up the Parzival theme again in his unfinished poem 'Mysteries' is connected with this. It is exactly the same problem, and you can truly go on to show how these things change. In this way you come to it along the inner path.

Why not perhaps also speak about *Goethe's Fairy Tale of The Green Snake and the Beautiful Lily?* You probably have done so, in fact. And why not (from the point of view of the images) compare the part about the kings with Johann Valentin Andreae's *Chymical Wedding* where you also find the king-image. If you go back from there you will arrive as a matter of course at the connections between the legends of King Arthur and those of the Grail. You will arrive at the esoteric element in the Grail legends and the King Arthur legends, and you will grasp the inner significance of the whole quality of the working of culture, when you see that King Arthur's Round Table set themselves the task of dispelling people's simple-mindedness and instinctive superstitions, and that the Grail Castle had set itself the task of helping people to spiritualise their lives and develop an inner core. You have the chance of bringing inner depth to the Parzival story and conversely of putting it into its historical setting. You will find indications of this in the lecture cycles, and also references to the story *Poor Heinrich*, where the motif of self-sacrifice can be historically explained. The moral conception of the world and the physical conception of the world were then one and the same, but this was immediately lost in the subsequent age. Something like *Poor Heinrich* could no longer have been written in the fifteenth century.

I have also made a comparison between *Parzival* and *Simplicissimus* by Grimmelshausen [1621–76]. In Christoffel von Grimmelshausen's day people had reached the point where they could not deal with the Parzival theme in any other way than humorously. You will find the form echoed in *Simplicissimus*. The history of literature shows this to be the case.

By the time we arrive in our present day things have become awfully covered up, but in spite of this we must discover them. It is a good thing if some of these matters are brought to light. Looking at the instruction Gurnemanz gives Parzival, the question can arise as to whether Gurnemanz still appears in the nineteenth century. Indeed he does. If you look at the situation, you see him in the person of Trast in Sudermann's *Ehre*. There is Trast, and there is Robert, the inexperienced simpleton. Trast is a proper Gurnemanz figure. You will find all the traits in caricature. Then again you will have a chance to point out that Robert is a kind of Faust, once again interpreted as a caricature, with Trast as a kind of Mephisto. Sudermann is an absurd fellow who takes everything

3. THE CURRICULUM AND METHODS FOR DIFFERENT AGES

into the absurd. This gives you the opportunity to show how tremendously superficial things became in the transition from the middle of the Middle Ages to modern times.

A question is asked as to why twelve religions are spoken of in Goethe's 'Mysteries'.

Dr Steiner: For the same reason that I spoke of twelve world conceptions in a lecture in Berlin. Goethe was not interested in following up these twelve religions. He knew that the twelve religions are connected with the twelve signs of the zodiac, and that is why he talked of twelve religions; not because he envisaged *a priori* that there are twelve possible religions. I myself would prefer to keep to Goethe's way of thinking. As soon as you start construing things, a philistine element creeps in. It is enough to give the number. Then you can quote examples. These things need not be made distinctly empirical

There are only twelve consonants, the others being variants of these. They do not appear as such in any language except Finnish, which has just the twelve consonants. The subject can be dealt with in this way. Now you only need to fill in the framework.

Meeting of January 17, 1923

A teacher: We are trying to awaken a religious mood, but there are difficulties with some children. X often ruins the lesson. He dislikes any kind of mood.

Dr Steiner: Yes, that is so. You can't do anything about it. But worse things can happen. You must make use of such a nuisance to lead over into seriousness.

A question about the Service for the older children.

Dr Steiner: It will be an Offering Service, for a Sunday that we shall decide on shortly.

A religion teacher asks another question.

Dr Steiner: For this question we need to return to something we have already talked about. Particularly with regard to matters relating to world outlook it is very important that our young people in the Waldorf School cease wanting endless discussions about this. The point is that we generate a mood which makes them realise that the teacher has something to say which the children can neither judge nor discuss. This is essential; otherwise things get hacked to pieces. Endless discussion drags things down. It must remain at the stage of asking questions, and the children, even those in Classes 10 and 11, must be conscious of the fact that they do all the asking of *you* and accept the answers you give. This is the situation as regards matters of religion and world outlook. The religion teacher needs to maintain his authority even when the children are beyond the age of puberty. We said this once before, in connection with the discussion periods. It has to be avoided. But you need not object to discussion when the children raise questions of conscience which you answer.

And here is another essential thing: the older children keep on coming back to the fact of your stressing that this is not a school for the production of anthroposophists. This is one of the matters that should be treated very seriously. You should make the children aware of the fact that they are being given the objective truth. And if this sometimes appears to be anthroposophical it cannot be helped, since what anthroposophy has to say is objectively true. The matter itself leads to it becoming anthroposophical. People must not go to the other extreme of saying that anthroposophy should not enter the school. It is in our school whenever it is objectively justified, whenever the subject itself leads to one such thing or another.

With things like *Parzival* it is better to discourage rather than encourage symbolism. Wagner's followers in Bayreuth have gone in for much more symbolistic nonsense than we have. We would never practise such rabid symbolism here. The main lesson must show Parzival as a man of the world, not as a monk. I really felt I should add this today. Of course some things are difficult for children.

You will do well to avoid symbolism as much as possible and, with the help of the historical background, keep to facts without becoming trite. Stick to facts, not symbols.

3. THE CURRICULUM AND METHODS FOR DIFFERENT AGES

The Child's Changing Consciousness and Waldorf Education

Dornach, April 22, 1923

At the same time we must also bear in mind that precisely in these matters an intensely religious element can be found. There is no need to have the name of the Lord constantly upon one's lips nor to call upon the name of Christ all the time. Better to adhere to the command, 'Thou shalt not take the name of the Lord God in vain.' Nevertheless, it is possible to permeate one's entire life with a fundamental religious attitude, with a most intensely Christian attitude. Then certain experiences of old, no longer known to modern intellectuality, will begin to stir in one's soul. They are experiences that are deeply rooted in human evolution, in the Christian development of humankind. For instance, teachers who in the depths of their souls are seeking the right stimulation for finding the appropriate forms of pedagogy, especially in these pathological-physiological areas, would do well to let themselves be inspired, time and again, by what radiates from the Gospel of Luke. (To modern ears such a statement must sound grotesque.) On the other hand, teachers who wish to instill in their pupils the necessary idealism for life would do well to find a source of inspiration by reading again and again in the Gospel of John. If teachers do not want their pupils to grow up into cowards, but into the kind of people who will tackle life's tasks with ebullient energy, they should look for inspiration in the Gospel of Mark. And those who are keen on educating the young to grow into perceptive adults rather than into people who go through life with unseeing eyes, may find the necessary stimulation in the Gospel of Matthew. These are the qualities which, in olden times, were felt to live in the different gospels. If our contemporaries were to read that in past ages the Gospel of Luke was felt to radiate a healing element in a medical sense, they would be unable to make anything of it. On the other hand, if they entered life as real pedagogues, they would begin to understand such matters again.

Faculty Meetings with Rudolf Steiner

Meeting of April 25, 1923

A teacher asks about the religion lessons in Class 12.
Dr Steiner: You should do the history of religion. You could give a survey of the religious evolution of mankind. Begin with ethnic religions, then national religions, and finally universal religions.

Begin with ethnic religions which are still entirely dependent upon ethnicity. Egyptian religions dedicated to local gods. Greece, too, had local gods all over the place. Take them progressively. First of all you have the religions where the worship is bound immovably to one place, the sacred place. Then you have the next kind, where the nomad's tent becomes the sacred place and the religious ritual becomes movable: this is when national religions arise. Then you have the universal religions, Buddhism and Christianity. No other religion could be called a universal religion.

A teacher enquires about the Apocrypha.
Dr Steiner: The children are too immature for the Apocrypha. The Apocrypha contain a lot that is more correct than what is in the gospels. We have always added what can be verified from the Apocrypha. The things conflict sharply. If the children are given a gospel, they must have all four. It is difficult to explain what the contradictions are about. If you take the Apocrypha as well, nothing tallies. I would advise taking the Acts of the Apostles.

A teacher asks a question about the religion lessons in Class 10.
Dr Steiner: After the Gospel of John there are several possibilities. Either Mark or selections from Augustine. Choose parts from the *Confessions* where he speaks more of religious matters.

3. THE CURRICULUM AND METHODS FOR DIFFERENT AGES

A Modern Art of Education

Ilkley, August 11, 1923

The faculty of personal judgment does not mature until the fourteenth or fifteenth year. Only then has the child developed to a point where the teacher is justified in appealing to his faculty of judgment. At the age of fourteen or fifteen he can reason things out for himself, but before this age we injure him, we retard his development if we continually enter into 'whys and wherefores'. The whole of later life is immeasurably benefited if, between the seventh and fourteenth years (approximately, of course), we have been able to accept a truth not because we see its underlying reason – indeed, our intellect is not mature enough for this – but because we feel that the teacher whom we revere and love holds it to be true. Our sense of beauty grows in the right way if we are able to accept the teacher's standard of the beautiful – the teacher to whom we give a spontaneous, and not a forced respect.

We shall rightly experience the good, so that we tread its path in later life, if we are not given a code of behaviour to follow, but have realized from the teacher's own warm-hearted words how much he loves a good deed and hates a bad one. His words can make us so warmly responsive to the good and so coldly averse to evil, that we turn naturally to the good because the teacher himself loves it. Then we grow up, not bound hand and foot by dogma, but filled with a spontaneous love for what is true, beautiful and good to the beloved teacher. If during the first period of school life we have learnt to adopt his standard of truth, beauty and goodness, a standard he has been able to express in artistic imagery, the impulse for these virtues becomes a second nature, for it is not the intellect that develops goodness. A man who has over and over again been told dogmatically to do this, or not to do that, has a cold, matter-of-fact feeling for the good, whereas one who has learnt in childhood to feel sympathy with goodness and antipathy to evil, who out of his feeling has preserved his enthusiasm for the good and his power to shun evil, has drawn right into his whole rhythmic organism the capacity to respond to the good and to be repelled by what is evil. In later life it is as though, under the influence of evil, he practically could not breathe, as if by evil the breathing and the rhythmic system were adversely affected.

It is really possible to achieve this if, after the child has reached his seventh year, we allow the principle of natural authority to supersede that of imitation which, as we have seen, must be predominant in the earlier years. Naturally, authority must not be enforced, for this is precisely the error of those methods of education that attempt to enforce authority by corporal punishment.

Ilkley, August 15, 1923

The ages of the children must always be taken into account in any teaching connected with religion, for infinite harm is wrought if ideas and conceptions are conveyed prematurely. That is why in our religion lessons in the Waldorf School the child is led, first of all, to an understanding of what is universally divine in the world.

You will remember that when the child first comes to school between the ages of seven and ten, we let plants, clouds, springs, and the like speak for themselves. The child's whole environment is living and articulate. From this we can readily lead on to the universal Father-principle imminent in the world. When the rest of the teaching takes the form I have described, the child is well able to conceive that all things have a divine origin.

And so we form a link with the knowledge of nature conveyed to the child in the form of fantasy and fairy-tales. Our aim in so doing is to awaken in him, first of all, a sense of gratitude for everything that happens in the world. Gratitude for what human beings do for us, and also for the gifts vouchsafed by nature – this is what will guide religious feeling into the right path. To unfold the child's sense of gratitude is of the greatest imaginable importance and significance. It may seem paradoxical, yet it is nevertheless profoundly true, that human beings should learn to feel a certain gratitude when the weather is favourable for some undertaking or another. To be capable of gratitude to the cosmos

3. THE CURRICULUM AND METHODS FOR DIFFERENT AGES

– even though it can only be in the life of imagination – this will deepen our whole life of feeling in a religious sense.

Love for all creation must then be added to this gratitude. And if we lead the child on to the age of nine or ten in the way described, nothing is easier than to reveal in the living world around him qualities he must learn to love. Love for every flower, for sunshine, for rain – this again will deepen perception of the world in a religious sense. If gratitude and love have been unfolded in the child before the age of ten, we can then proceed to develop a true sense and understanding of duty. Premature development of the sense of duty by dint of commands and injunctions will never lead to a religious inwardness. Above all else we must develop gratitude and love in the child, for then we bring up the child in the right way not only ethically and morally, but also as regards religion.

He who would educate in the sense of true Christianity must realize that before the age of nine or ten it is not possible to convey to the child's soul an understanding of what the Mystery of Golgotha brought into the world, or of all that is connected with the personality and divinity of Christ Jesus. The child is exposed to great dangers if we have failed to introduce the principle of universal divinity before this age, and by universal divinity I mean the divine Father-principle. We must show the child how divinity is imminent in all nature, in all human evolution, how it lives and moves not only in the stones, but in the hearts of other human beings, in their every action they do towards the child. The child must be taught, by the natural authority of the teacher, to feel gratitude and love for this universal divinity. In this way, precisely between the ninth and tenth years, the basis for a right attitude to the Mystery of Golgotha is laid down.

You see now why it is of such infinite importance to understand the being of man from the aspect of his development in time. Try for a moment to realize what a difference there is if we teach a seven- or eight-year-old child about the New Testament, or – having first stimulated a consciousness of universal divinity in the whole of nature – wait until he has reached the age of nine-and-a-half or ten before we pass to the New Testament as such. In the latter case, right preparation has been made and the gospels will live in all their supersensible greatness. If we teach the younger child about the New Testament it will not lay hold of his whole being, but will remain mere phraseology, just so many rigid, prosaic concepts. The consequent danger is that religious feeling will harden in the child and continue through life in a rigid form, instead of in a living form which through and through pervades his feeling for the world. We prepare the child most beautifully to take into himself, from the ninth and tenth years onwards, the glory of Christ Jesus if, before this age, he has been introduced to the principle of universal divinity imminent in the whole world.

This, then, is the aim of religion teaching given at the Waldorf School to an ever-increasing number of children whose parents wish it. The teaching is based on the purely human element and associated, moreover, with a certain form of ritual.

...

It was very difficult to introduce into this religious instruction the principle it is our aim to unfold in the Waldorf School, the principle of human development as such, for in religious matters today people are least of all inclined to relinquish their own special line. We hear a great deal of talk about a 'universal human' religion, but the opinion of almost everyone is influenced by the views of the particular religious body to which he belongs. If we rightly understand the task of humanity in days to come, we shall realize that the independent religion teaching that has been inaugurated by the Waldorf School is a true assistance to this task.

Anthroposophy as given to adults is naturally not introduced into the Waldorf School. Rather do we regard it as our task to imbue our teaching with something for which man thirsts and longs: a realization of the divine, of the divine in nature and in human history, arising from a true conception of the Mystery of Golgotha.

This end is also served when the whole teaching has the necessary quality and colouring. I have already said that the teacher must come to a point where all his work is a moral deed, where he regards the lessons themselves as a kind of divine office.

3. THE CURRICULUM AND METHODS FOR DIFFERENT AGES

This can only be achieved if it is possible to introduce the elements of moral instruction and religion into the school for those who desire it, and we have made this attempt in the religious instruction given at the Waldorf School – in so far as social conditions permit today. In no sense do we work towards a blind, rationalistic Christianity, but towards a true understanding of the Christ impulse in the evolution of mankind on the earth. Our one and only aim is to give the human being something that he still needs, even if all his other teaching has endowed him with the qualities of full humanity. Even if this be so, even if full humanity has been unfolded through all the other teaching, a religious deepening is still necessary if the human being, in an all-round way, is to find a place in the world befitting his inborn spiritual nature. To develop and unfold the whole human being and deepen him in a religious sense – this we have tried to regard as one of the most essential tasks of the Waldorf School education.

Faculty Meetings with Rudolf Steiner

Meeting of February 5, 1924

A request is made for a new curriculum for religion lessons in the upper classes.
Dr Steiner: We have outlined religion lessons for eight classes in two groups, Classes 1-4 in the lower group and the others in the upper group. A curriculum for religion lessons therefore exists at two stages. Are you now referring to a third stage?
It is asked whether it would be possible to give a specialised curriculum for the various classes, e.g. Classes 5, 8 and 12.
Dr Steiner: You can show me tomorrow how far I went previously.
A teacher asks about subject matter for religion lessons in Class 9.
Dr Steiner: Augustine, Thomas à Kempis.

Meeting of April 30, 1924

Dr Steiner: Religion lessons: on the whole we have already given the curriculum for these, as far as their character is concerned. There is really nothing specific I can correct in what you have given me. Nothing in particular needs changing. Surely we are now concerned with the upper classes. Class 12 should culminate in a survey of the religions of the world, not in order to give them the idea that none of them are genuine, but precisely in order that the various forms shall demonstrate their relative truth. That would be the ninth stage. In the eighth stage you should work at Christianity so that at the ninth stage it appears as the synthesis of the religions. In the eighth stage Christianity itself must be worked at. In the ninth stage a survey of world religions so that they culminate afresh in Christianity. At the seventh stage a kind of harmony of the gospels should be given. The presentation of Christianity in its essence and manifestation. They are familiar with the gospels by then. So, seventh stage the harmony of the gospels, eighth stage Christianity, ninth stage world religions.

[*At that time the independent religion lessons were arranged as follows. First stage: Classes 1 & 2; Second stage: Classes 3 & 4; Third stage: Class 5; Fourth stage: Class 6; Fifth stage: Class 7; Sixth stage: Class 8; Seventh stage: Class 9; Eighth stage: Class 10; Ninth stage: Classes 11 & 12.*]

Meeting of June 2, 1924

Dr Steiner: I should now like to hear something about your experiences with the teaching since Easter.
A question is asked about Bible stories in Class 3.
Dr Steiner: I have noticed some of you using Hebel's book.[9] My feeling is that the only book that can be used as a guide for Bible stories is the Schuster Bible, which is excellently structured. It is better not to take the actual texts of the stories but to tell them in your own way. Tell the children the stories in your own way. Use the book only to jog your memory and read up what you need

to find out. The new version has been bowdlerised, so the older version is still the best. However interesting the Hebel book is to read, if you want to read up what you already know, it is not suitable for the first lessons on the Bible, quite apart from the fact that the typeface of the present edition is abominable. So let us keep with the old Schuster Bible. Its structure is excellent. It is somewhat pedantic and Catholic, but *you* are not in danger of becoming too Catholic.

A religion teacher asks where the difference lies in dealing with Bible stories in the religion lesson and in the Class 3 main lesson.

Dr Steiner: You will learn a great deal about how to do it if you think about the principle underlying the fact that we have to take the Bible stories in these two different places. When we take them in main lesson in the context of the curriculum we treat them as something with an entirely universally human character. We simply make the children acquainted with the content of the Bible without giving it an especially religious colouring. We treat it as a secular subject, purely from the point of view that the Bible doubtlessly ranks as classical literature among other classical literature.

When dealing with the Bible in the religion lessons we take a religious point of view and put the Bible at the service of this independent element of religion. If we feel our way to this difference with tact, and do not go in for trivial enlightenment in the main lesson, then in working out this subtle difference there will be an extraordinary amount to be learnt for our own teaching skills. The difference lies in 'how' you do it, and this difference is extremely important.

What you have first told the children you then read to them in order to fix it. I certainly would not like to think that this Schuster Bible makes bad reading material. The pictures are quite humorous even, and not bad; slightly sickly, but not really sentimental. It is adequate as reading material for Class 3, and it can also be used for practising Gothic printing.

The Kingdom of Childhood

Torquay, August 20, 1924

In these independent religion lessons we first of all teach gratitude in the contemplation of everything in nature. Whereas in the telling of legends and myths we simply relate what things do – stones, plants, and so on – here in the religion lessons we lead the children to perceive the divine in all things. So we begin with a kind of nature religion, shall I say, in a form suited to all children.

Again, the children cannot be brought to an *understanding* of the gospels before the time between the ninth and tenth years of which I have spoken. Only then can we proceed to a consideration of the gospels in the religion lessons, going on later to the Old Testament. Up to this time [in the religion lessons] we can only introduce the children to a kind of nature religion in its general aspect, and for this we have our own method. Then we should go on to the gospels, but not before the ninth or tenth year, and only much later, between the twelfth and thirteenth years, should we proceed to the Old Testament.

Suggestions on methodology in the religion lessons

Mathilde Hoyer

In the words of Rudolf Steiner quoted above there are many suggestions as to method in the religion lessons. I shall here give a few general practical examples.

The teacher will always bear in mind the phase of development in which the children he is teaching find themselves. In their *first three years at school* the only possible method is to talk to them in stories, bringing them the tales or legends in a colourful and vivid way. One aspect of this is of course the need to prepare very thoroughly by working intensively on the great cosmic facts connected with human evolution. What one brings to the

3. THE CURRICULUM AND METHODS FOR DIFFERENT AGES

children should be externally as simple and plain as possible; but the preparation should encompass many worlds. In children up to the ninth year the colourful images presented to them will only work deeply enough into their being if there is a resonance of what the teacher himself has worked through, even though this remains in the background and is not expressed verbally. It is not with their ears alone that children of this age hear the sounds of speech and what those sounds are meant to convey by way of concepts; they perceive more than that. There is still something in them of their earliest infant years, about which Rudolf Steiner maintained that the whole child is like one great sense organ; the various organs are not yet differentiated, so all impressions are experienced by the *whole* body.

Something of this totality of experience still lives in the children, so that what they hear and see enables them to dip with their inner being into a vividly described world of pictures that mirrors true cosmic and human events. Just observe children of this age and see the phenomenon: how the head is held, and the limbs, how the unity of the whole child is at work in the eyes turned inwards to distant expanses, utterly abandoned to the experience; how the child claps and stamps in delight, how sorrow fills the eyes with tears and lets the arms drop, how the same eyes sparkle in anger as the small fists clench and the feet stamp; how the breath comes faster and is then held at moments of great tension, how the heart beats faster; faces flush and turn pale, and there is no doubt that something is happening which works not only into the soul but also deep into the bodily organs, bringing health or sickness, joy or pain.

If the content of the story is in harmony with cosmic events, if tension and relaxation, joy and pain alternate in a healthy way, and if by the tone of his voice and manner of his telling the teacher can arouse appropriate powerful feelings in the children before letting them abate again, then the breadth and holiness of religious feeling is woven which the children will need as a foundation for their later experiences. The effect of a harmonious balance satisfies the soul and makes the human being healthy.

Something is brought about which also happens in other contexts in our schools, in painting and in all the artistic activities of the children at this age; the child experiences something objective. The true events of cosmic and human evolution appear before the eyes of the children's soul in the garb of images that have colour and shape. The religion lessons during the first three years of school in particular should encompass wide and rhythmical pendulum swings of the soul powers. Let me give an example, merely as a suggestion, of how a lesson like this might be structured.

To begin the lesson the class speaks in chorus the verse given by Rudolf Steiner for the religion lessons:

> In those strong rays of sunlight
> That make the earth abound,
> In that bright green of grasses
> That springs from darkest ground,
> And where the stars inhabit
> Their homes in heavenly height,
> And in Man's eye where shineth
> The steadfast strength of sight,
> There do I feel the willing
> Of God, my spirit's light,
> To whom in soul's foundation
> My being I unite,
> That spirit, too, may be
> This man of earth in me.

These words should only be spoken when every child is ready to stand quietly and reverently. The teacher should carry this verse within him like a holy object and speak it with the children in a manner that lets them sense how he accompanies every word with true feelings and thoughts. A song might follow, perhaps the same as is sung in the Sunday Services. Then the children sit. Perhaps the teacher can now invite them to repeat verses or poems, or introduce new ones, so that together or singly they can be active and also accumulate a small collection of treasured verses or valuable sayings. Usually the children are very attentive in this, learn quickly and enjoy reciting together.

Then it can be a good idea to ask a few questions to remind them of the story told in the previous lesson. This encourages them to use their thinking powers. They are usually able to find the answers more accurately and quickly than the teacher expects, and their anticipation as to the continuing story, or a new one, builds up. Now, as the story is told, the children dip into the world of pictures in a way that allows their whole developing being to participate in spirit, soul and body. If the teacher is in good command of the story he will have a chance to observe now and then how it is affecting the children. He can regulate how he proceeds, so as not to awaken feelings that are too strong. In addition he can experience in his heart the joy of looking deeply through shining eyes and self-forgetful attitudes right down into the being of one child or another. Once in every religion lesson there should be an opportunity for there to be a moment in each child's soul when the All High is remembered in reverent awe and humility. But 'the children's relationship with the Christ-being should be protected'; the name should not be mentioned too often, and when it is, the teacher's reverent awe should show in the words he uses.

When a religion lesson is built up in this way it leads the children through singing and being active, through speaking and moving rhythmically and through thinking inwardly to enter with their whole being into experiencing the story.

Finally the whole lesson can be summarized in a verse that grows as though out of all that has gone before; or after a brief moment of total quiet the closing verse can be spoken by the children. This can be the same verse for many months so that they learn it through repetition; for example, 'I draw near to thee, O Lord,' or the Lord's Prayer, or another verse of a similar kind.

The way a religion lesson is built up will of course vary constantly, depending on the circumstances, but the basic structure remains the same. Repetition of the underlying structure will also strengthen children in their will.

The Children's Service on Sunday provides strong and healthy support for the religion lessons. Here the children experience their religion teacher holding the service as well. They sense that he stands before God in earnestness and humility, guiding their being to God's being in deep seriousness.

In the *middle* and *upper* classes of the Lower School a more meditative, contemplative mood can gradually come to the fore. The children may begin to ask questions; and some, especially the more intellectual ones, will listen to the stories with a degree of scepticism. Now the inner conviction that should live *between* rather than *in* the teacher's words will be what counts in going forward to meet the young doubters. The stories of people's lives, which the teacher often has to make up himself, or hunt for in literature (for instance, Tolstoy's stories), the lively descriptions of the three lower hierarchies at work, these things call for much tact and a great deal of effort on the part of the teacher. One is grateful if one succeeds through these stories in establishing a bridge leading from an experience of the sphere of the Father God to an experience of the sphere of the Son God which is, in fact, what underlies the growing child's religious experience at this age.

The essentials of the lesson's structure will not need to change much, but the manner of speaking and the expressions used will have to modulate. The children will need more and more space for their own considerations and their own ways of expressing themselves. This can be sensed especially as the festivals come round year by year. Some stories are told again each year, yet they are fresh every time, and call on the teacher to tell them in new ways as he experiences how the being of a class is changing. It is quite difficult to find suitable poems and verses for the children to learn by heart. These are an important content for the human soul right into old age. When they rise up in the soul on one occasion or another they bring with them a refreshing, rejuvenating element.

In this way the tree trunk developed in the early years will bear leaves of much splendour in the middle years before finally bursting into flower in the soul life of the children when the

3. THE CURRICULUM AND METHODS FOR DIFFERENT AGES

time comes for the gospel stories to be told and talked about. There is a danger of overdoing these wonderful shining stories and inundating the children with them. The element of 'caring for the children's relationship with Christ' has a special role to play here. One is now drawing near to the 'very highest', and any flippancy in the lessons can spoil a great deal. Right down to the way he speaks and gestures, the teacher must now stand before the youngsters in a manner that allows his own modesty and reverence for what he is telling them to shine forth in everything. He must be like an inner rock against which the rolling waves of adolescence break to no avail; kindly seriousness must smooth the waves to make room for solemnity and quiet listening. The material he offers must touch the deepest interest of the whole human being at this age. It is not only stories that are needed now, for now he must also seek out links with real life which are appropriate for the children's degree of 'maturity for the earth'. The inner drama of Christ's experiences on the earth, his battle with powers inimical to the life of soul, his sacrifice, his suffering figure, His death and the triumphant Risen One must stand before the children's soul with all the objectivity of human history. It is especially important now to create in every lesson a moment in which the presence of Christ can be tentatively sensed.

During the course of Class 8 the children are then led to their first experience of the Youth Service. Over the subsequent two years the pathway 'from childhood to youth' is sought and in the ups and downs of their soul life it can mean much to the youngsters to be able to draw direction and strength from the religion lessons and the Youth Service, which ought to take place every Sunday.

For *Classes 9 to 12* the religion teacher needs to be well-versed in 'every field of life'. There should be an alternation between 'reading in the book of spiritual revelation' and 'reading in the book of nature,' indeed in the book of the whole of life. Much is expected of the religion teacher not only in respect of the 'material' he presents to the youngsters but also with regard to *how* he treats and speaks to them. They want more than beautiful descriptions about uplifting events; they want to be given profoundly argued evidence and logically convincing answers to their questions. On their passage through the upper classes they should learn that there is no such thing as a pat answer, that every answer throws up new questions, and that solutions can only be found within the human being.

The religion teacher must learn to understand that without a view that encompasses both the world and the human being, without a view that comprehends the modern situation of both science and spiritual science, he will make no headway with *Classes 11, 12 and 13*. If between the ages of 16 and 19 the young people fail to find what they are looking for, they will try to sneak into lectures intended for adults only, or read the books of Rudolf Steiner for which they are not yet ready. With regard to these young, searching human beings one can feel like a secret guardian, a protector who constantly questions himself and who can only discover, from the way they react to what he has to offer, which guideline he must follow in the religion lessons. The teacher knows that fundamentally these young people long to be pious and devout. But their path to this must be discovered on the one hand from what is spiritual, and on the other from what is true in the ordering of universal facts. In this way the young people can be led to the 'human being' as such, both from the outside and from within, so that gradually then can also come to comprehend their own human being.

Together with the religion lessons, the Offering Service, taking place every Sunday if possible, can provide a strengthening and steady foundation for maturing young people. It can accompany them into life and offers even those who used to take part in the religion lessons, and who have long since left school, a chance to gather strength from the cosmic words of the service.

As life is today, it is especially difficult – far more so than it was before the Second World War – to bring about any kind of solemn, religious mood in Classes 7/8 to 12. One requires a penetrating knowledge of what is going on in the children's souls and also a gentle tact with which to discover what *these specific* children need. Much more than in the past it is necessary to address the facts as they are in real life, scientific or historical facts of the present time, biographies of eminent men and women. The religious facts should stand in the background in such a way that the young people's existential questions only begin to take shape rather than find immediate answers. These questions themselves push forward the inner development of the young soul. Many years may pass before this struggle with those questions reminds the individual of what he experienced in the religion lessons or the Offering Service, so that only much later does he discover what he then needs.

The religion teacher will find his most useful tools to be whatever he himself has worked through and achieved. The imponderable 'something' that results is what will have the right effect on children of every age. Searching and caring, wrestling and maturing with effort and courage will allow him to develop whatever he can bring to the children and young people taking part in the religion lessons when he feels responsible towards Rudolf Steiner and his work.

Rudolf Steiner's curriculum suggestions for the religion lessons

Hartwig Schiller

Over the six years during which Rudolf Steiner was able to work with the teachers in setting up and shaping the first Waldorf School he took many opportunities to make suggestions regarding the curriculum for the religion lessons. Gathered together, the details brought forward on so many occasions provide a very full and spiritually complete picture.

The curriculum for the religion lessons differs from all the other subjects in the way it came into being and also in the manner of its further development. On the one hand, in the faculty meeting of September 26, 1919 it was given a two-level structure that differed from the class divisions for the other subjects; only gradually were the lessons brought more in line with the normal division into classes. On the other hand, the curriculum for the religion lessons was always suited to a special degree of openness and variability, depending on the situation of the teacher and group of pupils concerned. In gathering together Rudolf Steiner's various suggestions for the religion lesson curriculum it appears appropriate to use the method of dividing the material into the three levels of which he himself spoke: the Lower School, the Middle School, and the Upper School:

◊ Classes 1–4 (Level 1)
◊ Classes 5–8 (Level 2)
◊ Classes 9–12 (Level 3)

This division involves a differentiation in teaching methods.

Historically there have also been other groupings for the religion lessons. These were transitional phases on the way from the original large groups comprising pupils from several classes to groups of a more manageable size. This went hand in hand with the careful widening of the circle of religion teachers which Rudolf Steiner handled personally. In the faculty meeting of June 14, 1920, for example, the following three levels were envisaged:

◊ Level 1   Classes 1–3
◊ Level 2   Classes 4–6
◊ Level 3   Classes 7–9

This was connected with a change in the organization of the lessons. Now the three classes of each level were taught together, and the groups embraced three rather than four classes.

A third division arose out of the meeting of April 30, 1924, resulting in every age-group being taught class by class.

3. THE CURRICULUM AND METHODS FOR DIFFERENT AGES

- ◊ Classes 1 & 2 Level 1
- ◊ Classes 3 & 4 Level 2
- ◊ Class 5 Level 3
- ◊ Class 6 Level 4
- ◊ Class 7 Level 5
- ◊ Class 8 Level 6
- ◊ Class 9 Level 7
- ◊ Class 10 Level 8
- ◊ Classes 11 & 12 Level 9

After this, as time went on, the 12-level structure gradually established itself and has remained in place ever since.

The present article, however, will depart from the current division into a curriculum for each separate class level. Instead it will follow Rudolf Steiner's basic design of a division into lower, middle and upper level with its stimulating principle of not following too fixed an arrangement. The purpose is simply to provide an overall view of Rudolf Steiner's various suggestions.

LEVEL 1

The lessons should take into account 'a kind of review of all kinds of conditions that existed before birth' which the children still experience 'as they approach their seventh year'. 'However, everything relating to reincarnation and karma should be omitted.'

Misguided worries about subject matter being 'too difficult' should be overcome. The 'sequence in which thoughts follow one another' is more important than 'absorbing the thoughts'.

The weekly verses from the Soul Calendar can certainly be included in the lessons at this level.

The Lord's Prayer. As regards praying, it is always important to bring the children into 'a mood of piety'. Similarly, we should not 'get the children to recite a lovely poem without first awakening in them a gentle smile, a joyfulness and delight'. Learning to pray is one of the most elementary tasks of the religion lessons.

The things and processes that surround human beings' should be discussed with the children in a way that 'arouses in them the feeling of spirit living in nature'.

In talking about the human soul, it is necessary to consider human development, 'the seriousness of the biography,' and 'the seriousness of death.'

The 'alternation between sleeping and waking' should be considered. This involves talking about how the soul imbues the whole body' when we are awake, and how the will begins to stir in the limbs. The body bestows the senses on the soul, so that it can use them as instruments. This should be given and discussed as the proof that spirit reigns in the physical realm.

Certain things should be avoided. Among these is 'any kind of superficial theorizing about expediency' such as, for example, 'Why do trees provide cork?' 'So that we shall have stoppers for champagne bottles. God has arranged things so that we shall have cork to make stoppers.'

Another thing to be avoided is the idea 'that the unknown provides proof of the spirit'. By allowing such ideas we encourage a tendency to believe in spurious miracles instead of cultivating a relationship with the spirit.

Metamorphoses. The transformation of caterpillar into butterfly. 'Poems about metamorphosis in plant and animal [can quite well] be used in religion lessons.' However, in doing so we must develop 'the feelings that move on from one line to the next'.

The inner picture that the human being 'with all his thoughts and actions stands in the midst of the whole cosmos.' God lives in whatever is alive in the human being. 'The divine lives in the leaf on the tree,' in 'the sun,' in 'the cloud,' in 'the river'. 'But the divine also lives in the circulation of the blood, in the heart, in what you feel, in what you think.' The human being is entirely 'filled with the divine'.

An awareness should be aroused in the children that 'because he represents God, because the divine is revealed in him, the human being is obliged to be a good person.'

This first level of the religion lessons has the task of awakening 'the feeling of God the Father'. Suitable in this connection are motifs from the Old Testament, among other things, 'if only they are treated correctly, the Psalms of David, the Song of Solomon and so on'. (This is mentioned as a concrete task for ten-year-olds.)

The Old Testament also contains the Ten Commandments, which demonstrate 'what a serious matter' this is.

'Older Catholic editions of the Bible' provide good examples 'of how to retell stories'. The Schuster edition for schoolchildren is recommended. The actual telling should always be a free rendering, with the book being used by the teacher only as an *aide-memoire* and for reading up stories. Rudolf Steiner's suggestions in this field led eventually to the production of the reader *Und Gott Sprach*.[10]

One error must be avoided: 'Do not imagine that you can leave Christ out; this must not be done.' The children must be given 'as tangible a picture of Christ as possible ... and this must be at all levels, [so that] the whole earthly life of Christ becomes the focus of attention.'

The most important aspects to be taken into account at this level are clearly spelt out. A 'feeling for the Father God should be awakened'. This involves an attitude of soul which reverently worships all that is lofty in creation, all that represents wisdom in the world, and which treats the whole of creation with respect. The growing children should be taught everything that 'can be revealed through the divine which exists in nature through wisdom'. The religion lessons are rather like lessons in a 'nature religion'.

Although the character of the religion lessons at the first level is based on the aspect of the Father God, one must not neglect to 'protect the child's personal relationship with Christ'. That is a task for religion lessons at all levels 'including the lowest'. Suitable ways and means involve cultivating 'a feeling for the seasons of the year,' following an 'ideal ritual element in the lessons,' and going more deeply through the feeling life into 'symbols and images'.

Especially important in this respect is the 'third religion

lesson', which is another name given to the Sunday Services for the children: remembering Christ, telling the Bible stories, and preparing for the Christian festivals during the course of the year.

Level 2

Talk with the children a great deal about 'the concepts of destiny, human destiny'.

This includes the difference between 'when something that happens to us is destiny and when it is a chance event'. These two experiences are distinguished at the feeling level, and they are used to 'teach the children gradually about the difference between finished karma, and new karma that is approaching'. The difference between what we have 'inherited from our parents, compared with what we have brought with us from a former life on earth'. Former lives on earth. 'Everything is brought in to help the children grasp both intellectually and with their feelings that the human being lives on the earth repeatedly.' The lessons should not theorize but should be quite practical, using examples.

For Classes 7, 8 and 9 'we could now begin to explain in theory, in a free way, life before and after death'. Suitable examples given are Goethe or Jean Paul.

The Laocoön Group as an example of the disintegrating human physical body. 'But this timidity' about what is happening 'must be elevated on to the religious level'.

Also 'take into account that the human being initially rises to the divine in three steps': firstly, 'to the divine that leads to the angel being' who accompanies individual human beings; secondly, one endeavours to explain that 'there are higher gods, the archangels', who lead whole groups of people or entire nations; 'thirdly, also bring in the concept of the Time Spirit as a divine being reigning over whole periods of time.' (Using the Old Testament, Moses, and then the sixth century as periodic steps.)

Only once these matters have been dealt with in the lessons do

3. THE CURRICULUM AND METHODS FOR DIFFERENT AGES

we 'move on to actual Christology'. Included here is the difference between pre-Christian and Christian times.

A study of the symptoms in history can deepen 'the urge for religion and the feeling for religion' by showing how leading to the Mystery of Golgotha 'there was first an ascending tendency, then a culmination with regard to certain events, and then a descent'.

When talking about the prophets, Michelangelo's figures can be brought in.

After a 'long period of preparation' for elementary Christology, 'one can progress to the gospels'. In doing this one should emphasize the way the four gospels complement one another while also giving different views. 'The greatest emphasis should be placed on the difference in feeling between the gospels.'

At both levels it is good for the children to learn suitable verses. At Level 1 the verses should 'stem primarily from the Old Testament', later on 'from the New Testament'. Do not on any account use the trite texts so often included in prayer books. Many of the 'verses we have in anthroposophy' are definitely suitable.

This level, too, was summarized by Rudolf Steiner in characteristic words: 'At the second level we have transformation: the human being recognizes the divine not through wisdom alone but through active love.' He also added that on the second level the slant is more towards 'historical religion'. At its core is the fact of Christ's appearance on the earth.

Another aspect of this second level is expressed in the indication that the lessons are a preparation for the Youth Service and that no other preparatory lessons are needed for this. Protection of the personal relationship with Christ is the aim, right up to the moment of death which is realized in the transition from childhood to youth.

Level 3

The description of the curriculum for the upper level is not as comprehensive as that for the other two. Nevertheless, lesson content for this age group was developed and described stage by stage in subsequent years during faculty meetings. Thus, after a summary of all the points he had made had been presented during the meeting of April 30, 1924 Rudolf Steiner was able to comment, 'Nothing much needs changing here.' When we list the various items we find that they do, in fact, amount to a curriculum that is quite differentiated for the various classes.

The crucial remark as to method was made during the meeting of June 21, 1922. This was the beginning of the fourth school year since the founding of the Waldorf School, during which the oldest class reached Class 11:

> ... take it in a way that calls on their power of judgment. The important thing, previously, was pictorial presentation; now the time has come when you really should try to work towards concepts. Deal with the problems of destiny in a religious way; guilt and atonement; Father, Son and Spirit. You work from pictures towards concepts, which will be a kind of study in cause and effect.

This describes the new kind of consideration and tone now appropriate for religion lessons in the higher classes if an impression is to be made on the pupils. It could be termed the method for Level 3.

Differentiation is now also called for. The girls need lessons that aim 'in some way to bring out what is aesthetic'. It is good if they can be made to 'feel glad that the world is imbued with the supersensible,' and if their imagination 'is richly filled with images ... which express how the world is filled with the divine and also which express what is beautiful in human beings who are good and morally upright.'

For the boys it is necessary to awaken inner pictures 'that point more towards the strength that lives in religious life and in ethical considerations'. Whatever is religious and beautiful should be guided towards the 'courage', 'the feeling of strength that shines forth from them'.

3. THE CURRICULUM AND METHODS FOR DIFFERENT AGES

In contrast to the suggestions he gave for the lower and middle level, Rudolf Steiner now gave curriculum indications for each class separately:

Class 9: Deal with life before birth and after death in a free way, and explain these theoretically. Give examples. Show the long-term cultural connections and use Goethe or Jean Paul as examples in connection with capacities deriving from life before birth. Study the Laocoön Group with its special sculptural forms as a way of observing how the ether body extricates itself from the physical. Elevate the timidity experienced when facing the disintegrating human body on to the religious level. Read from the works of Hermann Grimm. Acts of the Apostles with the addition of Luke's Gospel. In addition bring in St Augustine (see Class 10) and Thomas à Kempis.

It is assumed that after the lessons in Level 2 the pupils are familiar with the gospels. There now follows 'a kind of harmony of the gospels' with a depiction of 'Christianity in its whole being and manifestation'.

Class 10: John's Gospel, Mark's Gospel or those parts of Augustine's *Confessions* that are chiefly on the religious aspect. Work on the gospels should be brought to a kind of conclusion and summary. This should help the pupils experience the profounder harmonies of the gospels and should bring out 'Christianity as such'.

Class 11: Destiny question with the concepts of guilt and atonement. The Trinity of Father, Son and Spirit.

Parzival with the three stages of soul experience: innocence, doubt, blessedness. Possibly draw attention to the contemporary appearance of Dante's work, in which the threefold aspect should also be shown. In connection with Parzival avoid any kind of exaggerated symbolism. The mood should be worldly and not 'monkish'.

Christianity should be brought out in all these connections.

Class 12: History of religion. Survey of the religious evolution of humanity. Begin with ethnic religions (for instance, Egypt and Greece with their local gods) and move via national religions (for instance, the Hebrews) to universal religions (of which there are really only two, Buddhism and Christianity). What is genuine and good in the different religions should be emphasized.

Finally it should be shown that Christianity actually represents a synthesis of the various religions. The significance for humanity of the Christian religion should shine forth from the other religions.

Another indication (*Child's Changing Consciousness*, April 22, 1923) that applies to all the levels is the effect the gospels have on and through the teacher 'who gains a stimulus from them in the right way'.

Also fundamental are those indications which enjoin the teacher to cultivate the pupils' personal relationship with Christ. Equally important are those which encourage the teacher to make his lessons lively and filled with feeling and inwardness. It is perhaps in this connection that we may see Rudolf Steiner's seemingly contradictory statement (*Kingdom of Childhood*, Aug 20, 1924) that the gospels should be taken before the Old Testament.

May the independent Christian religion lessons finally overcome the old intellectualism which did not stop even at something as foreign to it as religion.

4. Division of the Religion Lessons into Class Groups and Weekly Lessons

From Rudolf Steiner's lectures and faculty meetings in chronological order

Faculty Meetings with Rudolf Steiner

Meeting of September 25, 1919

Dr Steiner: One-and-a-half hours religion a week is sufficient for each group; that is, two three-quarter of an hour lessons. It would be especially lovely if they could take place on Sundays, but no doubt that would be too difficult to arrange. You could also introduce the children to the Soul Calendar verses in these lessons.

Meeting of November 15, 1920

Dr. Steiner: Then we have these independent religion lessons for this class. How are they divided?
A teacher: We have nine classes in three groups.
Dr Steiner: Why have the classes become so large? If the dividing out is done properly there is no harm in large classes, but in your class they really are sitting on one another's heads. Herr U's class is too big and should be split: 73 children! They don't fit in the benches and they push one another off. This is disastrous. The naughtiest pupils were not there today. It is essential to split this class, isn't it? I certainly think so. And since so much depends,

particularly in these lessons, on keeping individual contact and being able to ask the various children questions as often as possible, you must have the opportunity of fitting in another two lessons and dividing off half the children.

There may be a problem with space, but this must be solved, otherwise these lessons are going to be wrecked.

Meeting of May 26, 1921

A class teacher says he has been attending his own class's religion lessons, to keep order, and he feels like a watchdog.
Dr Steiner: This one exception is perfectly possible from a certain point of view, and that is that we are maintaining what we reckon to be a part of our pedagogy. We must take it for granted that the teacher and his class belong together. As various classes are combined in the religion lessons I think it is perfectly possible for the teacher concerned to be present while another teacher is giving the lesson. There is hardly any other way of getting over this difficulty except by trying to make smaller classes.
A teacher: The children do not always participate properly because there are so many of them.
Dr Steiner: The groups are too big, which they ought not to be if the lesson is to have an intimate character.

Meeting of June 16, 1921

Dr Steiner: I have been trying hard to find someone for the religion lessons, but I cannot find anyone. It is essential to divide the children according to classes. I want to avoid making the religion lessons appear as a school subject.

Meeting of April 28, 1922

A religion teacher thinks that three quarters of an hour is too short for a religion lesson.
Dr Steiner: It is a blessing if you can have the religion lessons

4. DIVISION OF THE RELIGION LESSONS INTO CLASS GROUPS

more often. I cannot see why three quarters of an hour should be too little. I really think it is better if the children have these things called to mind twice a week. I should prefer it to be shorter still, but oftener.

Meeting of January 17, 1923

A religion teacher asks whether going on lecture tours is consistent with being a religion teacher.
Dr Steiner: If you are working in harmony, there is no difficulty.

Meeting of October 16, 1923

A teacher: Which lessons do we have to drop from now on in Class 12 because of the exam preparations?
Dr Steiner: Technology and handicrafts must sadly be dropped, also gym and singing. Eurythmy cannot be dropped. Freehand drawing remains. Reduce religion to one lesson, but do not put it in the afternoon. Class 12 will take part in only one of the joint religion lessons with Class 11.

5. Selecting Religion Teachers

From Rudolf Steiner's lectures and faculty meetings in chronological order

Faculty Meetings with Rudolf Steiner

Meeting of September 25, 1919

A teacher: Ought the religion lessons to be given by the class teacher?
Dr Steiner: One of us can take it on. It does not have to be the class's own teacher. It is not desirable to take someone from outside whom we do not know. We ought really to keep within the circle of our own teachers.

With 60 children we would take about 30 at a time, the four upper classes and the four lower classes as a group, perhaps. I will give you a curriculum for them. We must take great care over these lessons.

Meeting of March 6, 1920

Oehlschlegel had gone to America and his lessons had to be divided out among other teachers.
Dr Steiner: Herr Hahn will take on the upper group of the religion lessons. Then, including languages in Classes 3 and 5, he will have 25 lessons per week, so he will need to have some of this load taken off him.

5. SELECTING RELIGION TEACHERS

Meeting of July 31, 1920

Dr Steiner: Hahn will take Classes 1 to 3 together for the religion lessons, and likewise Classes 7 to 9 as one group.

How would it be if we were to invite Herr Uehli to join us?* It would be a solution. He hasn't got much time, but perhaps he could manage two lessons a week. So I would propose Herr Uehli for the group comprising Classes 4 to 6.

Meeting of September 22, 1920

Dr Steiner: The Sunday Service is fixed. Someone must be designated in place of Frau Koegel to lead the children in. Please make suggestions. It is something for which the person should feel a special calling. Is anyone going to volunteer? Would you like to do it with Fräulein Röhrle?

Meeting of November 15, 1920

Herr Uehli's group consists of 73 children and should be divided up.
Dr Steiner: Who else could give this lesson?
A teacher: I would gladly give it.
Dr Steiner: It ought to be someone who wasn't previously in a religious profession. You may have left it years ago, but you will not have lost your forms of thought. There is no one on the college of teachers. This is a difficult problem to solve, of course. You must also overcome what hinders you from bringing warmth into the lessons. Warmth! Warmth! I would even suggest A, for example, but I don't know whether he could adopt the necessary pedagogical quality. Suppose we try A? For who else in the anthroposophical movement could we suggest, at this time of crisis? There is nobody. People freeze a lot here!

I know of nobody else. No more can be put on the shoulders of

---

* Ernst Uehli was the editor of the weekly *Dreigliederung des Sozialen Organismus*.

the teachers here. Class 9 is so small that you can have real contact with the individual pupils.

Meeting of November 22, 1920

A teacher: I should like to ask whether we can also draw on ancient documents in the religion lessons.
Dr Steiner: Of course you can. Also things you make up yourself. I really think we ought to suggest to Herr A that he takes on half the religion class. Give him one half. You choose the ones you want to get rid of. Despite his age he will be just as young and fresh.
A teacher: Would Herr A also participate in the Services?
Dr Steiner: That will be necessary very soon.

Meeting of May 26, 1921

Dr Steiner: As religion teachers you do not belong to the school. You give the lessons as though you were a visiting clergyman from an anthroposophical church.

Meeting of June 16, 1921

Dr Steiner: I have been trying hard to find someone for the religion lessons, but I cannot find anyone. It is essential to divide the children according to classes. I want to avoid making the religion lessons appear as a school subject.

Meeting of June 22, 1922

Dr Steiner: There must be more women celebrants.

Meeting of October 28, 1922

A teacher: One of the religion lesson groups must be moved to the afternoon. Otherwise we would need another religion teacher.
Dr Steiner: The supply of religion teachers that can be had from

5. SELECTING RELIGION TEACHERS

the college of teachers is exhausted, partly because of time. And in Stuttgart there is nobody.

A young lady teacher: I would gladly give the lessons.

Dr Steiner: You must live here longer. One cannot make the decision oneself. Later on perhaps, if you feel the call. Just now you have not been in Stuttgart nor at the school long enough. It would not be possible.

[*To Fräulein Röschl*]: I would give it to you if you did not already have 17 lessons. I am afraid of your having too many lessons.

[*To another teacher*]: I was so little in agreement with your lesson that I could not take responsibility for it. As you disappointed me like this, you must forgive me if I speak quite frankly. After having participated in your lesson I cannot accept the responsibility. The religion lessons demand a high degree of responsibility.

A teacher: I would gladly take religion lessons.

Dr Steiner: Perhaps in five years' time if you work very hard. You have to grow into these things. You dare not take this subject without accepting the full responsibility. Imagine what it means, that religious life is being kindled in you. Religious life has to be kindled. It can be kindled in all kinds of ways. What about you, Herr Wolfhügel?

Herr Wolfhügel: I don't think it would work.

Dr Steiner: I think you could find your way into it. I have to deal with these things quite objectively. I believe I can vouch for you, and also for Herr Baumann.

A teacher: I would have to prepare for both lessons.

Dr Steiner: A lot of preparation is necessary, and atmosphere. I believe Herr Wolfhügel is afraid of the service. The religion lessons should be in your line. Seeing the kind of approach you have to teaching, these lessons should be up your street. But I am afraid it might overburden you.

The best thing would be if it could be someone belonging to the school. It could also be someone from outside. It is sad if there is no one here for it. It is a strange thing that nobody has yet felt the calling. I appreciate Dr E tremendously where science is concerned, but I would not give him a single class for religion lessons. I just wouldn't. But he knows very well how greatly I appreciate him.

Dr R (a theologian from outside the school) has a difficult time of it; he cannot even manage his own children. One of them gets the cane, a child who particularly needs careful handling. If they leave the boy for another six months at that school he will be ruined for life. His teacher canes him. His mother went to the teacher, wanting to speak to him, and started by saying, 'I would like to speak to you not as a teacher but as a mother to another human being.' 'Being talked to as a human being, I cannot put up with that.' She went to the headmaster and told him what the teacher had said. 'Well, you see, if you address a teacher in our school as a human being you are bound to get a rebuff, because that is an insult.'

That reminds me of a story which once happened at the Belgian-German border to a Russian lady travelling from London to Petersburg. She journeyed through Holland to the German border and wanted to behave in a typically Russian manner. The customs official came and said she should get down her suitcase. 'You see how heavy it is. Couldn't you help me?' 'I help you? How *can* you ask that of me? Am I a human being here? I am a royal Prussian official and not a human being. If you went to the market square I would be at your service and carry your case. But here in this place I am a royal Prussian official. So I am not allowed to lift it down.'

Herr Boy will probably be very suitable later on, but he has not been here long enough yet to take religion lessons. For these independent religion lessons you need more experience of anthroposophy.

Who gives lectures here in Stuttgart? Herr H would certainly have the spirit and everything else, but he has not got the temperament to be a teacher. There is no one among our anthroposophical friends either. The groups are very large. We shall have to group them differently until we find somebody. We are racking our brains in vain today. We are seeing the symptoms of our fundamental difficulties. Now that we have all these institutions – the Waldorf

5. SELECTING RELIGION TEACHERS

School and the Association for Independent Spiritual Life – we have put ourselves in a situation where we need capable people. We need these in various domains. Where teaching is concerned it is a matter of having the right person for the job. The teaching may possibly even appear to be less good sometimes, from a superficial point of view. But for this form of teaching the personality as such is also of tremendous importance. Perhaps there is someone among the doctors. I would give it to young N any day. There are several theologians I would gladly entrust these lessons to. I wouldn't give G any lessons at all for a long while. Writing bad articles is no prerequisite for being a good Waldorf teacher.

Meeting of December 5, 1922

A teacher: Shall Fräulein R and Herr W also take the service?

Dr Steiner: Both of them ought to celebrate the service. This is an understood part of the religion lessons. I would also like to tell you this. We have seen from experience that the religion lessons do not just consist of our teaching something in a lesson, not even if it has atmosphere, but that over and above this a definite relationship is established between the religion teacher and the pupils through the service. If someone else takes the service, then the pupils' own religion teacher loses the greater part of the imponderables on which his lessons are based. And conversely, anyone who celebrates a service without giving religion lessons is in a position that can hardly be justified. You can sooner justify giving the religion lessons without services than services without religion lessons. This raises the religion lessons above the level of mere theory. They are founded on a relationship between the religion teacher and the pupils. When I said you yourselves should decide, I meant the service.

A teacher: I still don't understand that.

Dr Steiner: Now that we have it all organised, the first thing I would ask a prospective religion teacher would be, can he do the service? But that would give you the wrong impression. If it were a matter of deciding whom of our friends here I consider suitable, you would be able to say, 'Only the ones I find eligible to take the service.' A number of people could be religion teachers, but the services could hardly be conducted by anyone else except the two just mentioned. You must not be angry that we have to be frank about this, and that everyone needs to know what he is considered suitable for. For the time being! It may change.

People must become ready for the Youth Service by themselves. This nonsense of separate confirmation lessons must stop. The Youth Service must come when they have reached a certain maturity. But this maturity cannot be taught. So it is not a matter of teaching but of sizing up the situation. That is why no special lessons can be introduced in preparation for confirmation. Also, only the person who takes the religion lessons should hold the Youth Service.

Meeting of June 19, 1924

A teacher asks about the choosing of new religion teachers.
Dr Steiner: You know, this fact could cause us greater difficulties some day than anything that has gone before. You know how we have sweated blood to find religion teachers. The teachers here are occupied with their specialist subjects and there are of course certain conditions attached to the teaching of religion. We might be in the position some day of having to apply to the Christian Community for a religion teacher for the school. I should put that off as long as possible, but it might become necessary.

Selecting religion teachers

Elisabeth von Kügelgen

In an endeavour to gain an overview of the criteria Rudolf Steiner mentioned during the faculty meetings with teachers as applying to the appointment of religion teachers the following points emerge.

5. SELECTING RELIGION TEACHERS

No fundamental difference is made between members of the college of teachers and others 'from outside', from the anthroposophical movement (Meeting of Nov 15, 1920). A prerequisite for such an appointment is that the person should be a member of the Anthroposophical Society, since 'the Anthroposophical Society actually provides the religion lessons and the Services' (Meeting of Feb 5, 1924). For example, when he was appointed in 1920, Ernst Uehli was a member of the editorial staff of the weekly journal *Dreigliederung des Sozialen Organismus*. Nevertheless, Steiner considered it desirable that a teacher should be appointed where possible, or someone who was 'good at teaching', and had the 'right temperament to be a teacher' and would seek to reach the pupils' souls. Anthroposophy must have become that person's inner life and the lessons must be suffused in warmth, a warmth emanating from the personal religious life of the teacher which he must have 'kindled' within himself. This is because 'the personality as such comes into consideration very strongly in these lessons'. Steiner stressed very clearly the special responsibility involved in this task. Indeed, he even mentioned that he himself must take responsibility for what went on in those lessons.

Once the Sunday Services had been established it became increasingly clear that a religion teacher must be someone who was capable of holding the services. Steiner even pointed out that not everyone had the kind of voice that would be suitable for the services. The person's way of speaking must be able to project warmth and kindled inner life. Standing before the children in the lessons and beside the altar was what created those 'imponderable' aspects that make the specific relationship of soul between teacher and pupils. Steiner called the matter of holding the services 'an understood part of the religion lessons' (Dec 5, 1922). Here religion will 'live' as a direct relationship with spiritual beings, where Christ is actually present.

This is not the place for a discussion of what 'entitles' a religion teacher to hold a service. However, I will permit myself to give three aspects:

1. Intensive work on *all* the faculty meetings in which Rudolf Steiner spoke about the religion lessons and/or the Sunday Services.
2. What is involved in truly bringing anthroposophy to life within oneself?
3. Another valuable key to this question would be words spoken by Rudolf Steiner and passed on to us by Herbert Hahn: 'If it [the service] could be held, this would be a first new link to our esoteric work that has been interrupted by the war.'

6. How the Religion Lessons Relate to Denominational Lessons

From Rudolf Steiner's lectures and faculty meetings in chronological order

Practical Advice to Teachers

Stuttgart, September 4, 1919

During the first year of elementary school we are after all dealing with children who are only just six or a few months older. When they are this age we can quite well practise the elements of drawing and painting with them, and also of music, and we can also do gymnastics and eurythmy. But if we give them religion lessons in the style of today we are certainly not teaching them religion but merely giving them a form of memory training, which is about the only good thing that can be said about it. For it is utterly nonsensical to speak to six or seven-year-old children about the concepts that play a part in religion. All they can do is memorize them. Memory training is of course quite a good thing but we must be aware of the fact that with these concepts we are presenting to the children all sorts of things for which they have absolutely no understanding as yet.

Discussions with Teachers

September 6, 1919

Now I probably do not need to tell you that even the subjects we have discussed so far will help the children develop an awareness of the spirit that permeates everything present in the world, an awareness that the spirit lives in our language, in the geographical elements covering the earth, and in the flow of history. When we try to sense the living spirit in everything, we will also find the proper enthusiasm for conveying this living spirit to our students.

Whenever we do this, we will learn to compensate our students for what the religious denominations have been doing to humanity since the beginning of the modern era. These religious denominations, which have never made the free development of the individual a priority, have cultivated materialism from various angles. When it is not permissible to use the entire content of the world to teach people that the spirit is active, religious instruction becomes a breeding ground for materialism. The various religious denominations have made it their task to eliminate all mention of spirit and soul from any other form of instruction because they want to keep that privilege for themselves. Meanwhile the reality of these things has dried up as far as the religious denominations are concerned, and so what is presented in religious instruction consists merely of sentimental clichés and figures of speech. All the clichés that are now so terribly apparent everywhere are actually due more to religious culture than to international culture, because nowadays the emptiest clichés, which human instincts then carry over into outer life, are being promoted by the religious denominations. Certainly ordinary life also creates many clichés, but the greatest sinners in this respect are the religious denominations.

It remains to be seen, my dear friends, how religious instruction – which I will not even touch on in these discussions, because that will be the task of the denominations in question

6. RELIGION LESSONS AND DENOMINATIONAL LESSONS

– will affect other types of lesson here in our Waldorf School. For now religious instruction is a space that must be left blank; these lessons will simply be given over to the religion teachers to do whatever they choose.* It goes without saying that they are not going to listen to us. They will listen to their church's constitution, or to their church gazette or that of the parochial school administration. We will fulfil our obligation to summon up the spirit for our children in all the other subjects.

The Spirit of the Waldorf School

Stuttgart, September 24, 1919

We have absolutely no need to assert anthroposophy, to assert it as a point of view by developing anthroposophical concepts and seeing to it that children learn these as they previously learned religion. That is not at all our task. We will continue with what we have already stated, namely that the Protestant and Catholic religion teachers shall teach the Protestant and Catholic religions. We will not set any obstacles in the way of the desire to give this religious instruction. We will keep our promises in this regard. We do not seek in any way to bring any new philosophical opinions into the school. We seek something else. Our viewpoint will result from spiritual science because it comes from human nature. We will pay attention to the way it develops human know-how, human capabilities, the way it directly flows into the human will. Our task lies in our pedagogical activities: how we act in a school, how we teach, how we plan the lesson and its goals, which teaching methods to use, how knowledge and philosophy affect the skill and capability of the teacher. These are our tasks.

---

* The independent religion lessons were not instituted until several weeks later.

Faculty Meetings with Rudolf Steiner

Meeting of September 26, 1919

Syllabus for the anthroposophical religion lessons for children.
Dr Steiner: These lessons would have to be given at two levels. If you really want to go into the matter of how to give an anthroposophical lesson that has a religious aim, you would have to take the concept of 'religion' far more seriously than is usually the case. The concept of 'religion' is usually falsified through all sorts of ideas about world conceptions getting mixed up with it that really do not belong there. This is why, via religious tradition, precisely the kind of thing that is not intended to be developed any further gets passed down from age to age. World outlooks of the past are preserved alongside those that have been further evolved. Such things assumed grotesque proportions in the age of Galileo and Giordano Bruno. It is almost a joke the way these things are still being justified even today. The Catholic Church excuses itself by saying that Galileo could not embrace the Copernican world conception because it was not recognised in his day – yet it was the Catholic Church itself that forbade it. I shan't go into that now; but what I want to mention is to impress upon you that religion has to be taken seriously as soon as we are concerned with anthroposophical matters.

Anthroposophy is a world conception, isn't it? And as such we do not want on any account to bring it into our school. But we want to develop in those children whose parents expressly ask for it, the kind of religious feelings the human soul acquires from this world conception. If we want to take anthroposophy as our starting point, however, we have to be very careful not to develop anything in a wrong way, and most of all we want to avoid causing premature development.

6. RELIGION LESSONS AND DENOMINATIONAL LESSONS

The Renewal of Education

Basle, May 6, 1920

Now you may well wonder how the religious element can play its part in all the different subjects mentioned. Especially with regard to lessons in history, geography, physics, mineralogy – for all these subjects are to be introduced around the twelfth year – the question arises, what part should the religious element play and how should this pervade the entire world picture and convey a feeling for the supersensible world? In this respect we find ourselves in a very difficult position. And here I have to tell you that owing to outer circumstances we are not able to be guided only by our educational principles. It is not yet possible for us to make direct use of what the science of the spirit has to offer to education. Nevertheless, what flows from its source can fructify education indirectly because it evokes artistic impulses, permeating the human being in such a way that he gains faculties and not only knowledge. It enables the teacher to tackle life more skilfully – if I may use such an expression – therefore making him more capable of developing the art of education. This is a characteristic feature of spiritual science. Today we must be content to bring at least this ability into the art of education.

In opening the Waldorf School it was not possible to found an ideological school. Therefore, right from the start, I insisted that religion lessons should be given by visiting ministers and priests, for the religion lessons are not part of our Waldorf curriculum. We do not interfere in their running in any way. Thus the Protestant religion teacher gives his religion lessons, as does the Catholic priest or whoever has been appointed to do so. The Jewish rabbi gives instruction in the Jewish faith, and so on. Public opinion will allow us only to use spiritual science indirectly for our teaching and, consequently, the Waldorf School could not be an ideological school.

Yet a strange situation has arisen. A number of our parents

approached us, explaining that they had not sent their children to any of the confessional religion classes because they themselves did not belong to any church. They declared that unless the Waldorf School would appoint its own teachers to give religion lessons based on broad human principles, they would not send their children to any religion lessons. And so we were obliged to offer anthroposophically orientated religion lessons to children whose parents had asked for them. There was no wish on our part to impose our religion lessons on any child or parent, for the Waldorf School is not an ideological school. We give these lessons only in answer to a request and not because we wish to promulgate anthroposophy as a world philosophy. There is a great difference between clamouring for anthroposophy as a world philosophy and making use of what it can offer to fructify the art of education.

We do not agitate for the content of anthroposophy, but we do clamour – if this is the right word – for the faculties it develops in those who are pursuing this path. Yet this brought about some surprising consequences, such as, for instance, that crowds of pupils left the religion lessons given by outside teachers in order to join those given by our own religion teachers. There was nothing we could do about it. This was a most unpleasant situation for me and quite a fatal one as regards our relations with the outside world. On the other hand, supporters of confessional religious instruction voiced their opinion that eventually their activities at the Waldorf School would be bound to come to an end. This, however, is not at all our intention, for the Waldorf School is not an ideological school. In the civilised world today it is not possible to develop a homogeneously comprehensive form of education. This will become possible only when a threefold social order allows the spiritual life to function independently. This is the reason why we have tried at least to fructify education through the science of the spirit. Nevertheless, since a special request has been made here, I shall speak during the last few evenings left to us about what the science of the spirit has to say regarding the teaching of history, geography and religion.

6. RELIGION LESSONS AND DENOMINATIONAL LESSONS

Die Verantwortung des Menschen

Dornach, January 22, 1921 (Trans. J.C.)

People's longing for great simplicity manifests in strange ways. I have just been handed a short report about a lecture given by the worthy Frohnmeyer on theosophy and anthroposophy.* It states, 'The entirely personal comparison with Christianity drawn at the end of the lecture reminds us of the well-known fact that these people are unfortunately rather put out by something truly great being so simple.' What is meant is that the anthroposophists are put out by something great being simple, which is how Pastor Frohnmeyer would like to see it since he cannot be bothered to make an effort to recognize how very many different facets great things have. It is always a matter of putting things in the right words, and that is our task: to put things in the right words! Of course we do not have to overdo it by immediately going on at length about how human beings are instructed prior to being born, or that in earlier times people were born into groups whereas nowadays people are not born into groups. We can make it our task, however, to imbue ourselves with these truths, and then, depending on how things are being done, we shall be sure to find opportunities for showing people that we are just as unlikely to take dogma into the Waldorf School as we are to bring together in economic groups or associations those people who subscribe to a particular dogma.

    This has been adhered to in our Waldorf School in Stuttgart, where you can see that we had no interest at all in teaching anthroposophy to the children. What we want is a *method* of teaching that can only be derived from anthroposophy. This is an entirely objective matter. Meanwhile, for those children who want it, or whose parents want it, we make sure that the Catholic priest comes to give them Catholic religion lessons; and the Protestant pastor comes to the Waldorf School to give Protestant religion

---

* Leonhard Johannes Frohmeyer was a contemporary author and lecturer of the history of the Theosophical Society.

lessons for those who want them. We do not obstruct these people in any way.

However, in this day and age, when so many parents, especially working class people, have no intention of sending their children for any kind of religion lessons, whether Catholic or Protestant, we felt we should ask them whether they would like them to have non-denominational religion lessons born of anthroposophical education. It has turned out that very many children who would otherwise grow up without any religion, and would not consider attending denominational religion lessons, now come to the anthroposophical religion lessons which do not, though, teach anthroposophy, but which are born out of anthroposophy. The fact that these children are now more eager in their attendance at the religion lessons than are those being taught by the Catholic or Protestant priest is something we can do nothing about. Perhaps the Catholic or Protestant priest can.

It is certainly not our fault that gradually more and more children have switched over to the other religion lessons, to the extent that the Protestant religion teacher has been heard to say, 'Soon there will be no one left in my lessons; they've all gone.' That was last year. Were we concerned to approach the children with any kind of dogma? We have no interest in doing such a thing. If our method succeeds in breaking through the veil in the way I have described, we know that the children will be having the best lessons possible, namely those which they received in the spiritual world before they descended to the earth.

There are certainly some religious denominations that are very interested in muddying these lessons and preventing them from emerging. Those who are in a position to compare the peculiar relationship that exists today between the papal encyclicals and what happens in the spiritual world, know full well that the divine religion lessons enjoyed by the children before they descend to the earth bear no relation to the lessons certain denominations want to give them here. This is especially noticeable with regard to the Catholic church because through its rituals and ceremonies it can still exercise some supersensible influence, unlike the Protestant

6. RELIGION LESSONS AND DENOMINATIONAL LESSONS

church. The supersensible influence in question can, however, come to the fore in various ways, so that one has to admit, perhaps it diverges from the truth as the result of an error; or perhaps something is an error because it is the opposite of the truth.

Soul Economy

December 30, 1921

As mentioned before, it is not at all our aim to teach an ideology in the Waldorf School, though such a thought might easily occur to people upon hearing that the anthroposophists have founded a new school. Our aim is to carry insights gained through knowledge of anthroposophy right into actual teaching.

This is the reason why I did not mind handing over the responsibility of giving religion lessons to representatives of the various religious denominations. Religion, after all, represents the very core of a person's world outlook. And so, in our Waldorf School, a Catholic priest was asked to give Catholic religion lessons to pupils of his denomination, and a Protestant priest was given the task of teaching the Protestant religion lessons. When this decision was taken, we were not afraid of being unable to balance any outer influence brought into the school by these priests, influence which might not be in harmony with what we were trying to do. But then a somewhat unexpected situation arose. For when our friend Emil Molt founded the Waldorf School, most of our pupils came from the homes of the workers employed at his factory. Among them were many children of atheistic parents, children who, had they been sent to another school, would not have received any religious instruction at all. Gradually among these children – in the way such things happen when one is dealing with children and their parents – there arose the wish that they, too, should receive some form of religion lessons. And this is how our 'independent' – that is, non-denominational – religion lessons came about. They were given by our own teachers, just as the other religion lessons were given by the respective priests. These teachers were recognized by us as religion teachers of the Waldorf curriculum. In this way, anthroposophical religion lessons were introduced in our school. These religion lessons have come to mean a great deal to many of our pupils, but particularly to the children of the factory workers.

However, all this brought specific problems in its wake, for anthroposophy is there for the adult. If, therefore, the teacher wants to bring the right content into his anthroposophical religion lessons, he has to create it anew, and this is no mean task. For it means a remoulding and transforming of anthroposophical content in order to make it suitable for the various age groups. In fact, this task of changing a modern philosophy to suit young people occupies us a great deal. It mean working in depth on fundamental questions such as, what is the effect upon pupils of our using certain symbols? Or how do we deal with the imponderables inherent in such a situation?

Faculty Meetings with Rudolf Steiner

Meeting of June 22, 1922

Dr Steiner: I have told the Protestant religion teacher that I should also like to come to his lesson, but he said he would need more time to consider it. I shall also ask the Catholic teacher.

We make a mistake in this realm, too. I noticed it in the way the pupils answered when they were asked what their confession was. The manner of their answer showed that we still do not have unity in the school. We must realise that we have to be serious about the fact that when we give the Catholic children to the Catholic priest we have to feel that this is only the introduction of a confession which is not closely connected with the rest of the curriculum. We must always remember this, otherwise an unpedagogical principle will creep into the school. It strikes me

6. RELIGION LESSONS AND DENOMINATIONAL LESSONS

that perhaps we give the Catholic children the impression that we are not glad to see them. It was very indicative the way the other children made faces. This brings disunity into the school. We must overcome this. We must be serious about treating the different religious confessions with proper respect. I am much less concerned about whether or not the religion teacher gets the feeling he is a foreign body in our school. I do not think you are particularly concerned about the Catholic and Protestant children's religion lessons. I do not think you are much concerned at all.

A teacher: The child says, 'He doesn't tell us anything about Jesus.'

Dr Steiner: That confirms it even more. It is even more worthwhile for children like that. It is deplorable. It is not a good thing that she ought to be good. It is often like that and we have to accept it. It would help if you were to pass the time of day with the Protestant religion teacher. When we were standing in the passage today I was wondering when Herr S would introduce me to the vicar. But he didn't. This is another of the imponderable factors. That sort of thing is not good.

I do not consider it harmful for the children to go to mass. It would not be a bad thing to encourage them to go. I should not object if the Protestant children also took a liking to attending mass. Mass is definitely not a bad thing. It is impersonal, and it is the content of it which produces the effect. You can altogether disregard the priest who is celebrating it. Mass is very impressive. But it means more to see mass as such than to take part in High Mass. With the *Missa Solemnis*, as it is done in church, the mass is drowned in pomp. Mass consists solely of the four parts: the Gospel, the Offertory, the Transubstantiation and the Communion. It is most effective of all when there is just the priest with two servers. It is not possible for us to encourage the Protestant children to go to mass, yet they would certainly get something from it. I am extremely sorry that I did not go into more classes.

The Spiritual Ground of Education

Oxford, August 24, 1922

Since, under present conditions, we have had to make compromises, it has not been possible to give religious instruction to many of the children. But we can give the children a moral training. We start, in the teaching of morality, from the feeling of gratitude. Gratitude is a definite moral experience in relation to our fellow human beings. Sentiments and notions which do not spring from gratitude will lead at most to abstract precepts as regards morality. But everything can come from gratitude. Thus, from gratitude we develop the capacity for love and the feeling for duty. And in this way morality leads on to religion. But outer circumstances have prevented our figuring among those who would take the kingdom of heaven by storm – thus we have given over the instruction in Catholicism into the hands of the Catholic community. They send to us in the School a priest of their own faith. Thus the Catholic children are taught by the Catholic priest and the Protestant children by the Protestant pastor. The Waldorf School is not a school for a philosophy of life, but a method of education.

It was found, however, that a certain number of children did not belong to any denomination and would get no religious instruction under this arrangement. But, as a result of the spirit which came into the Waldorf School, certain parents who would otherwise not have sent their children to any religion lessons requested us to carry the teaching of morality on into the sphere of religion. It thus became necessary for us to give a special religious instruction from the standpoint of anthroposophy. We do not in these anthroposophical religion lessons teach anthroposophy, rather we endeavour to find those symbols and parables in nature which lead towards religion. And we endeavour to bring the Gospel to the children in the manner in which it must be comprehended by a spiritual understanding of religion, etc. If anyone thinks the Waldorf School is a school for anthroposophy

6. RELIGION LESSONS AND DENOMINATIONAL LESSONS

it shows he has no understanding either of Waldorf School pedagogy or of anthroposophy.

As regards anthroposophy, how is it commonly understood?' When people talk of anthroposophy they think it means something sectarian, because at most they have looked up the meaning of the word in the dictionary. To proceed in this way with regard to anthroposophy is as if on hearing the words, 'Max Miller of Oxford,' a person were to say to himself, 'What sort of a man can he have been? A miller who bought corn and carted the corn to his mill and ground it into flour and delivered it to the baker.' A person giving such an account of what the name of Miller conveyed to him would not say much to the point about Max Miller, would he? But the way people talk of anthroposophy is just like this, it is just like this way of talking about Max Miller, for they spin their opinion of anthroposophy out of the literal meaning of the word. And they take it to be some kind of backwoods sect; whereas it is merely that everything must have *some* name.

Anthroposophy grows truly out of all the sciences, and out of life, and it was in no need of a name. But since in this terrestrial world people must have names for things, since a thing must have some name, it is called anthroposophy. But just as you cannot deduce the scholar from the name Max Miller, neither can you deduce from its name anything about what anthroposophy really is. We simply bring the anthroposophical religion lessons into the School where they stand side by side with the other religion lessons.

I mean no offence in saying this, but others have taken us to task about it. The anthroposophical religion lessons are increasing: more and more children come to them. And some children have even deserted the other religious instruction and come over to the anthroposophical religion lessons. Thus it is quite understandable that people should say, 'What bad people these anthroposophists are! They lead the children astray so that they abandon the Catholic and Protestant religion lessons and want to have their religious instruction there.' We do all we can to restrain the children from coming, because it is extraordinarily difficult for us to find religion teachers in our own sphere. But, in spite of the fact that we have never arranged for this instruction except in response to requests from parents and the unconscious requests of the children themselves, to my great distress I might almost say, 'The demand for this anthroposophical religious instruction increases more and more.' And now thanks to this anthroposophical religious instruction the School has a wholly Christian character.

The Child's Changing Consciousness

Dornach, April 18, 1923, Answers to Questions

A question regarding religious instruction is put.
Dr Steiner: A misunderstanding has arisen through my preliminary remarks about the child's development in regard to his religious impulses. So far nothing has been said in my lectures about religious instruction itself, because it was only today that I began to talk about the practical application of Waldorf pedagogy. What I had told you was that there exists a kind of physical-religious – I called it 'bodily-religious' – relationship between the child and his environment. Furthermore, I said that what the young child exercised – simply on account of his organism – entered the sphere of thinking only after puberty, approximately after the fourteenth to fifteenth year. What manifests at first physically-spiritually, and then continues its existence in a hidden way until it re-emerges in the thinking realm only in approximately the fifteenth year, I compared with an underground stream surfacing again on lower ground. In the case of the adult, religion is closely linked to the thinking sphere. However, if pedagogy is to be in line with the child's natural development, careful preparation for what will emerge later on already has to be made during an earlier stage.

So the question arises: bearing in mind these laws of human

6. RELIGION LESSONS AND DENOMINATIONAL LESSONS

development, how are the religion lessons to be planned for pupils between the ages of six and fourteen? This is one of the questions that will be dealt with in the coming lectures.

However, in anticipation I would like to say that we must be clear about the fact that the religious element is simply inborn in the child, that it is part of the child's being. This is revealed particularly clearly through the child's religious orientation up to the change of teeth, as I have already described it. What has eventually become religion in our general civilization – taken in an adult sense – is something that naturally belongs to the world of ideas, or at least depends on ideation for its content, which, true enough, lives mainly in the adult's feeling-realm. Only after the fourteenth year does the adolescent gain the necessary maturity for appreciating the ideational quality and content of religion. For the class teacher (Classes 1–8) the important question therefore arises, how must we arrange our religion lessons? Or, more precisely. to which part of the child must we appeal through our religion lessons during this age from the seventh to the fourteenth year?

During the first life period, up to the change of teeth, we directly affect the child's physical organization through our educational influence. After puberty, fundamentally speaking, we work upon the powers of judgment and upon the adolescent's mental imagery. During the intervening years we work upon the child's feeling-life. This is the reason why we must lead the child into this period through a pictorial approach, for pictures work directly upon the inmost feeling life. The powers of mental imagery mature only gradually, and they have to be prepared well before their proper time. What we now have to do in our religion lessons is to appeal, above all, to the children's life of feeling, as I will describe it tomorrow in regard to other subjects. The question is: how do we do it?

We work upon the children's *feelings* by letting them experience feelings of sympathy and antipathy. This means that if we develop the kind of sympathies and antipathies between the seventh and fourteenth year that will finally lead to proper judgments in the religious sphere, we will be acting rightly. Thus we avoid the attitude of 'Thou shalt' or 'Thou shalt not' in our religion lessons, for it would be of little pedagogical value for a child of this age. Instead we arrange our lessons in a way that will induce feelings of sympathy for what the child is meant to do. We do not explain our real aims to the children. Using the pictorial element as medium, we present to the children what will fill them with feelings of sympathy in a heightened sense, also a religious sense. And, likewise, we try to induce feelings of antipathy towards what they are not meant to do.

In this way, on the strength of feelings of right or wrong, and always through the pictorial element, we try to lead the young pupils gradually from what is divine-spiritual in nature, via the divine-spiritual in the human being to their making the divine-spiritual their own. However, all this has to reach the child through his life of feelings, certainly so up to Class 8. What we must avoid is a dogmatic approach, or setting up moral commandments. We must do all we can to prepare the child's soul for what, later on, is to develop into the adult faculty of forming sound judgments. In this way we shall do far more for the child's future religious orientation than by giving him religious commandments or set articles of faith at an age when he is not yet ready for them. By clothing our content in images – thus preparing the ground for what in later life will emerge as religious judgment – we prepare for our pupils a possibility of grasping through their own spirituality what they are meant to grasp as their own innermost being, namely their religious orientation. By appealing to the children's feeling-life in our religion lessons – that is, by presenting our content in pictures rather than through articles of faith or in the form of moral commandments – we grant them the freedom of finding their own religious orientation in later life. It is of immense importance for young people, from puberty right into their twenties, to have the possibility of lifting up, out of their own strength, into conscious individual judgments, what they first received – given with a certain width and many-sidedness – through their life of feeling. It will enable them to find their own way to the divine world.

It makes all the difference whether children, during the age of authority, are brought up in a particular religious belief, or

6. RELIGION LESSONS AND DENOMINATIONAL LESSONS

whether, by witnessing the teacher's underlying religious attitude, they are enabled 'to pull themselves up like a plant on its tendrils' in order to develop their own morality later in life. Having first found pleasure or displeasure in what finally condensed itself into a 'Thou shalt' or 'Thou shalt not' attitude, and having learned to recognize through a pictorial contemplation of nature how the human soul becomes free through an inner picture of a divine-spiritual weaving in nature and in history, a new stage is reached, where the young people's own images and ideas can be formed. In this way the possibility is given of receiving religious education out of the midst of life itself. It is something that becomes possible only after puberty has been reached.

The point is that future stages have to be prepared for in the right way, that is, on the basis of the correct insight into human nature. In my lectures I have used the comparison of the river that disappears underground to resurface lower down. During the first seven years the children have an inborn religious attitude. This now enters the depths of their souls, becoming part of them, to resurface in the form of thinking only with the arrival of puberty. During the second life period we must work into the depths of the pupils' souls through what is revealed to our individual insights. In this way we prepare them for growing into religious adults. We impede this process if we do not offer our pupils a possibility of finding their own religious orientation later on. In every human being there exists an individual orientation towards religion which, after the fifteenth year, has to be gradually won. It is our task to prepare the ground so that this may happen in the right way. And that is the reason why at this age we have to treat the religion lessons in the same way as lessons in the other subjects. All of them have to work upon the child's soul through the power of imagery; they have to stimulate the child's feelings. It is possible to introduce a religious element into every subject, even into maths lessons. Anyone who has some knowledge of Waldorf teaching will know that this statement is correct. A Christian element pervades every single subject, mathematics included. This fundamental religious current flows through the entire education.

But because of prevailing circumstances we have felt it necessary to come to the following arrangement with regard to religious instruction. (And here I should like to point out once more that the Waldorf School is not an ideological but a pedagogical school, where the fundamental demand is that our teaching methods should be in harmony with the child's nature. Hence we have neither the wish nor the intention of teaching our pupils to become anthroposophists. We have chosen anthroposophy to be the foundation simply because we believe that a real pedagogy can flow from it.) Our Catholic pupils are taught by visiting Catholic priests, and our Protestant pupils by visiting Protestant ministers. Waldorf pupils whose parents are free-thinkers and who otherwise would not receive any religious instruction at all, are given religion lessons by our own teachers. However, the surprising fact has emerged that nearly all our Waldorf pupils now attend the religion lessons given by the Waldorf teachers. They have all flocked to the 'independent' religion lessons, lessons which, in their own way, comprise what permeates all our teaching.

These independent religion lessons have certainly caused us a great deal of concern. With regard to these lessons, our relationship to the school is quite an unusual one. We consider all the other subjects as a necessary and intrinsic part of our education from the point of view of the principles and methods resulting from anthroposophical research. But in the case of the independent religion lessons we feel ourselves to be on the same footing as the visiting Catholic or Protestant teachers. In this sense, Waldorf teachers who give religion lessons are also 'outsiders'. We do not wish to have an ideological or confessional school – not in an anthroposophical sense either. Nevertheless, our anthroposophical methods have shown themselves to become very fertile ground precisely for these independent religion lessons, in which we do not teach anthroposophy, but which we build up and form according to the methods already characterized.

Many objections have been raised against these independent religion lessons, not least because so many children have changed over from the denominational to the independent religion lessons.

6. RELIGION LESSONS AND DENOMINATIONAL LESSONS

This has brought many other difficulties in its train, for, despite our shortage of teachers, we had to find among our existing staff one new religion teacher after another. It is hardly our fault if pupils desert their denominational religion lessons because they wish to join the independent religion lessons. The obvious reason is that the visiting religion teachers do not apply Waldorf methods, and the right methods are always the decisive factor, in religious instruction too.

Answer to a further question regarding religion lessons.

Dr Steiner: The characteristic mark of Waldorf education should be that all educational questions and problems are considered only from the pedagogical angle, and religion lessons are no exception. The Reverend X surely will admit that the two directions mentioned, namely the possibility of replacing religion lessons by moral tuition on the one hand, and that of denominational schools on the other, have been raised from quite different viewpoints. The suggestion of replacing religious instruction by lessons in moral conduct is usually made by people who wish to do away with religion altogether and who are of the opinion that religion has become more or less superfluous. On the other hand, a tendency towards religious dogma easily brings about a longing for denominational schools. Neither of these are pedagogical points of view.

In order to link them a little more precisely to the pedagogical aspects, I would like to ask what it is that constitutes the pedagogical point of view. It is surely the presupposition that a human being is not yet complete during the stage of childhood or youth – something only too plain to see. The child has to grow gradually into a full human individual, which he will achieve only during the course of life. This implies that all potential and dormant faculties in the child should be educated – and here we have the pedagogical point of view in its most abstract form.

If now someone who represents the purely pedagogical outlook resulting from insight into human nature declares that the child comes into the world with an inborn kinship to the religious element, and that during the first seven years his body is steeped in religion, only to hear a call for replacing religion lessons by lessons in ethics, it must strike him as if the adherents of such an idea were unwilling to exercise a human limb, say a leg, because they had concluded that the human being needs to be trained in every respect except in the use of legs! To call for the exclusion of an essential part of the human being can only stem from a fanatical attitude, but never from a real pedagogy. In so far as only pedagogical principles are being defended and pedagogical impulses scrutinized here, the necessity of religious teaching certainly follows from the pedagogical point of view. This is the reason why we have established the independent religion lessons for those children who, according to the regulations of the school authorities, would otherwise have been deprived of religious instruction, as already stated.' Through this arrangement, and through the fact that all the children belonging to this category are attending the independent religion lessons, there is no pupil in the Waldorf School who does not have religious instruction. This procedure has made it possible for us to bring back the religious life into the entire school.

To speak about the proper cultivation of the religious life at school and to counter the effects of the so-called 'religion-free enlightenment', by appealing to the inborn religious disposition in the young may be the best way forward towards a religious renewal. I consider it some kind of success for the Waldorf School to have brought religion to the children of religious dissidents. The Catholic and Protestant children would have received religious instruction in any case, but it really was not at all easy to find the appropriate form to enable us to open this subject to all our children. It was striven for only from the pedagogical point of view.

A Modern Art of Education

Ilkley, August 15, 1923

The principle of the 'universally human', which I have described in its application to the different branches of teaching, is expressed in Waldorf School education in that this school does not in any sense

6. RELIGION LESSONS AND DENOMINATIONAL LESSONS

promulgate any particular philosophy or religious conviction. In this connection it has, of course, been absolutely essential – above all in an art of education derived from anthroposophy – to remove from the Waldorf School any accusation of being an 'anthroposophical school'. Most emphatically it can be nothing of the kind. New efforts must be made every day to avoid falling into anthroposophical bias – shall I say – on account possibly of over-enthusiasm or honest conviction on the part of the teachers. The conviction, of course, is there in the Waldorf teachers because they are anthroposophists. But the fundamental element of the Waldorf School education is the human being himself, not the human being as an adherent of any particular philosophy.

And so – with the various religious bodies in mind – we were willing to come to a compromise demanded by the times and in the early days to confine our attention to the methods to be adopted in a 'universally human' education. To begin with, all religious instruction was left in the hands of the pastors of the various denominations – Catholic teaching to Catholic priests, Protestant teaching to Protestant ministers. But a great many pupils in the Waldorf School are 'dissenters' – as we say in Central Europe – that is to say they are children who would receive no religious instruction at all if this were limited to Catholic and Protestant teaching. The Waldorf School was originally founded for the children of working people in connection with a specific industrial enterprise – although for a long time now it has been a school for all classes of the community – and for this reason a large majority of the children belonged to no religious confession.

As often happens in schools in Central Europe, these children were being taught nothing in the way of religion, and so, for their sake, we have introduced an 'independent' religious instruction. We make no attempt to introduce theoretical anthroposophy into the School. Such a thing would be utterly wrong. Anthroposophy so far as been given for adults; one speaks of anthroposophy to adults, and its ideas and conceptions are therefore clothed in a form suitable for them. Simply to take what is destined for adults in anthroposophical literature and introduce that, would have been to distort the whole principle of Waldorf School education. In the case of children who have been handed over to us voluntarily for independent religious instruction, the whole point has been to recognize from their age what we should give them in the way of religious instruction.

Let me repeat once again that the religious teaching given at the Waldorf School – and corresponding services are connected with it – is not in any sense an attempt to introduce an anthroposophical conception of the world. The ages of the children are always taken into fullest account. As a matter of fact the great majority of the children attend, although we have made it a strict rule only to admit them if their parents wish it. Since the element of pure pedagogy plays an important and essential part in this independent religious teaching – which is, of course, Christian in the deepest sense – parents who wish their children to be educated in a Christian way, and also according to the Waldorf School principles, send them to us. As I say, the teaching is Christian through and through, and the effect of it is that the whole School is pervaded by a deeply Christian atmosphere. Our religious instruction makes the children realize the significance of all the great Christian festivals, of the Christmas and Easter festivals, for instance, much more deeply than is usually the case nowadays.

Faculty Meetings with Rudolf Steiner

Meeting of February 5, 1924

Dr Steiner: When the Waldorf School was founded great importance was attached to making it an institution independent of the Anthroposophical Society. It is logically quite in accordance with this that the denominational religion lessons are arranged by the religious communities and the independent religion lessons by the Anthroposophical Society and that the Anthroposophical Society stands in the same relation to their independent religion lessons as do the other religious communities to theirs. The

6. RELIGION LESSONS AND DENOMINATIONAL LESSONS

Anthroposophical Society, in fact, gives the religion lessons and the services. We can say this with full justification whenever we are accused of being an anthroposophical school.

Human Values in Education

Arnhem, July 24, 1924

In regard to religious instruction, the Catholic children are taught by a Catholic priest, and the Protestant children by a Protestant clergyman; and only because there are in Germany a great many people who do not belong to any church are we obliged to arrange for independent religion lessons as well. Otherwise these children would have had no religion lessons at all. I have great difficulty in finding teachers for these religion lessons that are over-full. There is no inducement whatever to persuade the children to attend, for we want to be an entirely modern school. All we want is to have practical and fundamental principles for the instruction and education. We have no wish to introduce anthroposophy into the school, for we are not a sect; we are concerned with what is universally human. We cannot prevent the children from leaving the Protestant and Catholic religion lessons and coming to our independent religion lessons. It is not our fault that they come. So we are obliged to ensure that these independent religion lessons can continue.

The Kingdom of Childhood

Torquay, August 20, 1924

How should religious instruction be given at the different ages?
As I always speak from the standpoint of practical life, I have to say that the Waldorf School method is a method of education that is not meant to bring into the school a philosophy of life

or anything sectarian. Therefore I can only speak of what lives within the Waldorf School principle itself.

It was comparatively easy for us in Württemberg, where the laws of education were still quite liberal. When the Waldorf School was established we were really shown great consideration by the authorities. It was even possible for me to insist that I myself should appoint the teachers without regard to their having passed any state examination or not. I do not mean that everyone who has passed a state examination is unsuitable as a teacher! I would not say that. But still, I could see nothing in a state examination that would necessarily qualify a person to become a teacher in the Waldorf School.

In this respect things have really always gone quite well. But one thing was necessary when we were establishing the school, and that was for us definitely to take this standpoint: we have a 'method-school'; we do not interfere with social life as it is at present, but through anthroposophy we find the best method of teaching, and the school is purely a method-school.

Therefore, I arranged from the outset that religious instruction should not be included in our school syllabus, but that Catholic religious teaching should be delegated to the Catholic priest, and the Protestant teaching to the pastor, and so on.

In the first few years most of our pupils came from a factory background (the Waldorf-Astoria cigarette factory), and among them we had many 'dissenting' children, children whose parents were of no religion. But our educational conscience of course demanded that some kind of religious instruction should be given them also. We therefore arranged 'independent religion lessons' for these children, and for this we have a special method.

7. The Sunday Services

*From Rudolf Steiner's lectures and faculty
meetings in chronological order*

Faculty Meetings with Rudolf Steiner

Meeting of March 6, 1920

There are questions about the arrangements for the Sunday Services and the music for them.
Dr Steiner: The Sunday Services are only for those children who go to the independent religion lessons. They are a substitute offered to those children and parents who have no religious ceremony. The service should be concluded with music; some special instrumental music. We will only invite guests when I am present.

Meeting of June 14, 1920

A question is asked about the people allowed to attend the Sunday Service.
Dr Steiner: This really is a difficult situation. It was not the intention that people other than parents should come. Of course, once you start with that it is difficult to draw the line. What shall we do? Why were non-parents admitted? If you allow K to come you have no reason to refuse other members. Where does it start and where does it stop? Aunts will come anyway. There have been other disturbances caused by strangers interfering in the running of the school. What I found most disturbing was people interfering in matters of discipline who had nothing to do

with the school. I have no objection if admission to the service is strictly limited to parents. Brothers and sisters and aunts also to be excluded. We are not holding the service for *them*. There is no limit to it. Only the parents or those the staff recognise as the responsible guardians.

A teacher asks whether an old member could come to the Service.

Dr Steiner: She will readily stay away if you explain it to her properly. The trouble is that the moment you allow someone to come who has no child at the school, it is difficult to draw the line. The Anthroposophical Society would be the place where exceptions have to be made. Or we leave it as it is.

A teacher: That has just proved unworkable.

Dr Steiner: Perhaps you can cope with these exceptions on one or two occasions, but they will increase.

A teacher: It is not a school matter as such. After all, it is separate from the school.

Dr Steiner: The Sunday Service is a part of the school as a whole. It is one detail of it, just like saying we would arrange a lesson for a certain handicraft, or something. That would also be a special matter that could exist within the framework of the school without being a part of the general school. We ought to keep it like that, otherwise we will have these troubles. People asked me recently how one should set about starting a Sunday Service for anthroposophical youth in H. At the present moment, when attacks are being made from all sides, that is the stupidest thing to do. That would be asking for trouble, for Herr L to set himself up and perform a ritual service for anthroposophical children. He has already obtained permission to see it. I definitely do not want to have anything to do with arranging a Sunday Service outside the framework of the school. It only makes sense through the fact that a number of children in our school have religion lessons founded on anthroposophy, and the Sunday Service is for *them*. Other children could be admitted, but we could never admit anyone who is not at the school.

A teacher: Then we must leave it at that.

Dr Steiner: We can leave it as it is. There will be exceptions then,

7. THE SUNDAY SERVICES

but I really cannot see how you are to refuse anyone else if you tell Frau G she may come. Herr Leinhas ought also to be refused admission, but he is in the Waldorf School Association. Perhaps that would mean he has a kind of right: anyone who belongs to the school.
A teacher: Can teachers' wives be counted as part of the school?
Dr Steiner: Of course they cannot be admitted. If they have no children they are not entitled to come.

Meeting of September 11, 1921

Dr Steiner: The theological course is due to take place in Dornach from 26 September to 10 October. Hahn, Uehli, Ruthenberg and Mirbach will be going to it. The independent religion lessons will have to drop out and other lessons would have to be given instead. If Dr Schwebsch were free at this time it would be interesting for instance if he could do some history or history of art that was suitable for this age group. Or it could be something else. Would you please now bring forward any questions that have arisen.

Meeting of November 16, 1921

A teacher: The wish has arisen to have a special Sunday Service for teachers.
Dr Steiner: We have discussed something like this before. I would need to know whether the request is general.
A teacher: The wish has been expressed.
Dr Steiner: Something very fine could come of it, of course. I can well imagine that a common striving is possible. The way to set about it would not be so easy to find. Who would take it? Let us assume you would elect the people to take it and they would alternate. That sort of thing is very difficult. There would have to be a very strong common bond of will among you. Who would take it?
A teacher: It never occurred to me that this would be a point of contention. We can't allow ourselves to harbour ambitions.

Dr Steiner: If each of you has a different opinion as to who would take it well, it is difficult. You will all agree that it should be taken by someone who does it well, that is obvious. But then the story changes. It's like the Stockerau anecdote [a place very year Vienna]. A Viennese was asked whether it was a long way to America, to which he replied, 'It isn't far to Stockerau, but after that it's a long way!'

A teacher: Ought it to be confined to one person?

Dr Steiner: If not, then every week you have to bother about who does it well.

A teacher suggests Herr N.

Dr Steiner: You ought to do a secret ballot.

A teacher: Surely what matters is that we have it.

Dr Steiner: Certainly. It is as difficult a matter as electing the pope.

A teacher: I would accept any of the others.

Dr Steiner: Let us think about how to do it. I would never venture, myself, to nominate the person to do it.

A teacher: One of the three gentlemen who takes the services for the children.

Dr Steiner: If everyone accepts them without even inwardly turning a hair. A service is either a matter of mere form, in which case you can introduce and do it together, or it is a ritual, which must be taken very seriously. There must not be any ill-feeling.

Another teacher speaks on the subject.

Dr Steiner: I don't follow any more. I'm completely baffled. A religious ritual is esoteric. A religious ritual is the most esoteric thing you can possibly imagine. I suppose what you were saying is that you cannot vote democratically where ritual is concerned. Once a ritual has been started, it can be fostered by a college of teachers, of course. For that, the college would have to be unanimous.

A teacher: I had understood that no sort of authority ought to be exerted over individuals.

Dr Steiner: That is what I have in mind. Just the way the ritual for the children was introduced. That wouldn't at all be the task of the Waldorf School.

The question is, whether something of this kind, that has to be

7. THE SUNDAY SERVICES

built up so carefully from a certain point of view, isn't something that cannot easily be started or fostered as a common cause by the college of teachers as such.

Let us presume that you are unanimous to start with. Then the next time you would have to confine yourselves to taking on to college only those teachers who are also in agreement with you. An esoteric community is only for people who are really esoterically united. A religious service is possible in esoteric circles only if it is meant to have significance, otherwise you must have a kind of mass. But for this again you need an esoteric element serving the ones who receive it unesoterically, for you cannot read mass without priests. Members of an esoteric community should be united through the esoteric content.

There is a request for esoteric meetings.

Dr Steiner: That would be very difficult to start. Up till now I have always had to stop anything I have started. You know that years ago there was plenty of esoteric activity, but I had to stop it, because it was being disgracefully abused. People were simply making free with esoteric matters in public, and they were becoming distorted. Nothing as disgraceful has ever happened in this regard, and it was in our esoteric movement that it occurred. Esoteric matters of any kind, even if they were disreputable, have always been treated confidentially. This has always been so, down the ages. But a system of cliques broke out in the Anthroposophical Society, and these cliques lord it over everything, unfortunately even esoteric matters. It isn't the anthroposophical cause as such that has first consideration; it is the interests of the cliques that conflict with this all the time. The anthroposophical movement is splitting up into a multitude of cliques. In some respects it is worse than in the non-esoteric world, isn't it. I don't want to show lack of understanding for the history of the thing, but just ask yourselves what we see throughout the external bourgeois world among real philistines. If a privy councillor is transferred from one town to another, he has to make polite inaugural visits to all the people of the opposite camp. But what happens in the Anthroposophical Society is this: when someone goes to a town where there are several groups, it can happen that he may be delighted at the thought of attending them all. But if he has been to one, the next one shows him the door. The naive fellow imagined he would be welcome everywhere. There really are towns where a number of anthroposophical groups treat one another in this way.

Esotericism is a painful subject in the anthroposophical movement. Constant harping on what has happened in the past is not the only thing. It is a fact that in every new article that Kully writes in the *Birseck-Post*, you can see how well informed he is about all the latest events that have happened over here, right down to the most trivial matters.* We really ought to be able to find a way.

A teacher: Can we find a way?

Dr Steiner: We really have to find a new way of doing it. You will have seen the wonderful movement that has led to the theologians course. That was run in a very esoteric way. It involved the founding of a ritual in the highest sense of the word. You can see from that how united we were.

At any rate I will be able to think about the matter, and try to come to an understanding of your needs. Isn't the children's Sunday Service an esoteric experience for the individual who attends it, irrespective of whether he is a child or not?

After all, you must realise that the layman has a minister – Protestantism doesn't contain any esotericism any more – the minister has a deacon, who in his turn has a bishop, and it goes on like that right up to the pope. But the pope, too, has a father confessor. This shows how the human situation is changing. The rigid acceptance of principle is essential. The father confessor is not superior to the pope, but in certain circumstances he can reprimand the pope and lay a penance upon him. The Roman Church, of course, gets into the most terrible situations.

I will think the matter over.

---

* Rev Max Kully (1878–1936) was a Catholic priest who wrote articles attacking anthroposophy in local newspapers, including the *Birseck-Post*.

7. THE SUNDAY SERVICES

Soul Economy

December 30, 1921

I have already mentioned that we found it necessary to give some kind of anthroposophical religion lessons to our pupils. Soon afterwards, arising out of these lessons, another need was felt which led to the introduction of a Sunday Service for our pupils. This service is in the nature of a ritual in which the children take part with deeply religious feelings. We have found that such a ritual, performed before the children's eyes every Sunday morning, has greatly deepened their religious experience.

The Sunday Service had to be extended for the sake of those pupils who were about to leave our middle school. In Germany it is the custom for pupils of this age to be confirmed in a special ceremony which signifies their having reached a stage of maturity at which they are ready to enter life. We, too, have made similar arrangements for a ceremonial which, as experience has shown, has made a lasting impression upon our pupils.

Faculty Meetings with Rudolf Steiner

Meeting of June 22, 1922

A teacher raises a question regarding the Sunday Services.
Dr Steiner: We ought to have five services. But there is the difficult question of individuals and rooms.
A teacher: We would need long curtains.
Dr Steiner: They can be as long as they are now. We are anyway not going to attain total perfection, so we might as well do it like that.

There must be more women celebrants.

I cannot give you the gospel text here. I will certainly do it but there is not time to do it here. I will try to give you the text as soon as possible.

Meeting of December 5, 1922

A teacher: The religion teachers would like to keep the room they have been using for the Sunday Services exclusively for that purpose.

Dr Steiner: I agree to that. The important thing is to have the right atmosphere for those for whom the service is being held. This arrangement would best serve that purpose.

A teacher: Shall Fräulein R and Herr W also take the service?

Dr Steiner: Both of them ought to celebrate the service. This is an understood part of the independent religion lessons. I would also like to tell you this. We have seen from experience that the religion lessons do not just consist of our teaching something in a lesson, not even if it has atmosphere, but that over and above this a definite relationship is established between the religion teacher and the pupils through the service. If someone else takes the service, then the pupils' own religion teacher loses the greater part of the imponderables on which his lessons are based. And conversely, anyone who celebrates a service without giving religion lessons is in a position that can hardly be justified. You can sooner justify giving the religion lessons without services than services without religion lessons. This raises the religion lessons above the level of mere theory. They are founded on a relationship between the religion teacher and the pupils. When I said you yourselves should decide, I meant the service.

A teacher: I still don't understand that.

Dr Steiner: Now that we have it all organised, the first thing I would ask a prospective religion teacher would be, can he do the service? But that would give you the wrong impression. If it were a matter of deciding whom of our friends here I consider suitable, you would be able to say, 'Only the ones I find eligible to take the service.' A number of people could be religion teachers, but the services could hardly be conducted by anyone else except the two just mentioned. You must not be angry that we have to be frank about this, and that everyone needs to know what he is considered suitable for. For the time being! It may change.

7. THE SUNDAY SERVICES

People must become ready for the Youth Service by themselves. This nonsense of separate confirmation lessons must stop. The Youth Service must come when they have reached a certain maturity. But this maturity cannot be taught. So it is not a matter of teaching but of sizing up the situation. That is why no special lessons can be introduced in preparation for confirmation. Also, only the person who takes the religion lessons should hold the Youth Service.

A teacher asks about the artistic furnishing of the Service

Dr Steiner: I will bear it in mind. I think it would be good if you could get hold of a harmonium. We want to think carefully about the furnishings. There is nothing to be said about the form of the spoken words except that we still lack the gospel texts. We could develop the musical aspect more, and also the picture decorations. There is of course another matter to be considered, but perhaps this has already been done. And that is, how does it stand regarding the attendance of the whole staff?

Meeting of January 17, 1923

Dr Steiner [*in answer to a question about the service for older children*]: It will be an Offering Service, for a Sunday that we shall decide on shortly.

A Modern Art of Education

Ilkley, August 15, 1923

A service is held every Sunday for the children who are given this independent religious instruction, and for those who have left school a service with a different ritual is held. A certain ritual, then, similar in many respects to the mass, but always adapted to the age of the child, is associated with the religious teaching given at the Waldorf School.

Faculty Meetings with Rudolf Steiner

Meeting of February 5, 1924

A question is asked whether Dr Steiner could give some specifications regarding seasonal additions to the services: colours, or something of that sort.

Dr Steiner: In the case of the Youth Service, which is going to be given at Easter, it is part of the whole purpose of this service. But I do not know what you have in mind. One might be preoccupying the children with a suggestive mood. That is not good as long as they go to school. It robs them of their naivety. Children up to a certain age should remain naive with regard to what takes place unconsciously, shouldn't they? So we should not present a whole calendar of the year. It would present them with a suggestive atmosphere. Up to a certain age they should remain naive regarding things of that kind. Similarly, you could not ask a toddler who has just learnt to walk, to step with the vowels or the consonants. It is only for the Offering Service that different parts of the gospels are allotted. Where the Youth Service is concerned I think we can proceed more concretely. We do not follow the seasons in the Offering Service either. It does not go according to the calendar. Chronology applies only to what is read. From Christmas till Easter we certainly try to give the story of the Birth and of the Passion, but after that the main intention is that the listeners get to know the gospels. I do not think the choice should be according to the calendar.

The Kingdom of Childhood

Torquay, August 20, 1924

This then is how you should think of the independent religion lessons. We are not concerned with the Catholic and Protestant instruction: we must leave that to the Catholic and Protestant pastors. Also every Sunday we have a special form of service for those who attend the independent religion lessons. A service is held and forms of worship are provided for children of different ages. What is done at these services has shown its results in practical life during the course of the years; it contributes in a very special way to the deepening of religious feeling, and awakens a mood of great devotion in the hearts of the children.

We allow the parents to attend these services, and it has become evident that this independent religious teaching truly brings new life to Christianity. And there is real Christianity in the Waldorf School, because through this naturalistic religion during the early years the children are gradually led to an understanding of the Christ Mystery when they reach the higher classes.

8. How the Religion Lessons and the Services Relate to the Christian Community

From Rudolf Steiner's lectures and faculty meetings in chronological order

Faculty Meetings with Rudolf Steiner

Meeting of December 5, 1922

Dr Steiner: The matter has two aspects. There is a strong question of whether we are permitted to precipitate matters. The movement for religious renewal with its ritual, could have the makings of something very great in this direction. On the other hand I have heard the following criticism in a town in which this movement for religious renewal is already at work: 'Today we have the situation where there is a religious community of a hundred members consisting only of anthroposophists who are becoming sectarian.' So you see, it has its dangers. These do exist. 'Members who have not yet joined are urged to do so.' The movement for religious renewal was intended for those outside the Society. You must realise that these things have two aspects and that, above all, those who are now our anthroposophical friends, within and outside this school, must see it as their mission to help those people who might otherwise go astray to see straight. The more sublime a thing is, the greater the dangers to which it is exposed. This should not be taken lightly. Before it has been conclusively proved that this movement for religious renewal is right and true,

8. RELIGION LESSONS AND THE CHRISTIAN COMMUNITY

let nothing be done that might make it look as though it were not to be respected.

The best thing at present is to do the services for the children with the kind of warmth and sincerity that conveys a serious attitude without becoming oppressive, yet keep them as simple as possible.

Rudolf Steiner's talk with the religion teachers at the Stuttgart Waldorf School on 9 December 1922

From shorthand notes taken by Karl Schubert.
No full record was kept. (Trans. J.C.)

Dr Steiner: We can now talk about the future arrangement of the religion lessons and the practices in the Sunday Services. Perhaps it would be good if you could first tell me what you would like to say separately from the full meeting of teachers, since you wanted this meeting of religion teachers only.
A teacher (X) expressed thanks, saying that as the group of religion teachers they wanted to feel they were a community and also to have a sense of being led by common viewpoints. They had been concerned about how to share out the services. In this connection there were difficulties because of the fragmented timetable.
Dr Steiner: Yes, this depends on the number of pupils. How have you done it so far? You have had four Sunday Services.
A teacher (X): We have taken it in turns, so that all the religion teachers have also held both the Sunday Service and the Youth Service. This has meant that the children who came to the Sunday Services were not always the pupils of those holding the service.
Dr Steiner: This is of course not the most desirable way of doing things. It would be good if the one giving the lessons were also the one holding the service. For those who have already attended it, the Youth Service can then only be a repetition. Every child attends the Youth Service for a first time. Thereafter, so as not to

go backwards, the next Sunday Services could be a repetition of the Youth Service. This can be something quite short.

A teacher (X): There were 14 to 16 pupils in each group.

A teacher (Y): At Easter Classes 8a and 8b will join as well.

Dr Steiner: You could manage this number in only two services.

A teacher (Y): There were 60 children on the first Sunday, 30 on the second. They don't all come.

Dr Steiner: Not all the children come. You could stick to having four services only. But you should see to it that each child has his own teacher celebrating the service on some Sundays, though not all. If not every Sunday, then at least on some Sundays each child should have his own teacher holding the Service.

A teacher (X): Raises the question of whether a personal counselling situation that might have arisen could be passed on when a new teacher took over a class.

Dr Steiner: The fact of the matter is that you yourself applied for this.

A teacher (X) states which classes he would be most willing to hand over: Classes 7 and 11.

A teacher (Z) says that he would most like to take on an Upper School class, but that in the case of Class 11 one would be destroying something that wanted to come into being.

Dr Steiner: The distribution arose out of the situation as it was at the time. Y has Classes 8a and 8b. There is the least need to change anything in his case. V has Classes 9, 6a, 6b, 5a, 5b. X has Classes 4a, 4b, 7a, 7b, 10 and 11. W has 2a, 2b, 3a, 3b; W has 1a and 1b. So this is the situation – how many lessons have you got, Herr V? W has 19 lessons; X has 20; U has 20. So we can consider W, X and V to be overburdened, especially in the case of X.

A teacher (X): I have felt these lessons to be a beautiful part of my work.

Dr Steiner: The important thing is that this work should be carried out as thoroughly as possible. The other work with the classes must not be allowed to suffer. You cannot manage to handle 20 lessons. This is not something that I would say to the handwork teacher, but in the case of the religion lessons it is not

8. RELIGION LESSONS AND THE CHRISTIAN COMMUNITY

possible. Twenty lessons are too many. We might consider 16 or 17 to be normal. Which classes would Z take over?
A teacher (Z): Perhaps Class 9.
A teacher (X): Perhaps W could take on Class 7.
Dr Steiner: So this would mean that Z would take on Class 9 and W Class 7.
A teacher: V would rather give up Class 5 than Class 9.
Dr Steiner: Let's do it like this: Z can take on Class 9. Class 5 would be difficult for Z. Then all we need to do is work out the groups.

The Services would involve a rota that ensured that all the pupils had their own religion teacher for the Sunday Service. It would be a good thing anyway if the teachers could join the pupils who come to the Sunday Services. Suppose V is taking the service for Classes 6a and 6b. If other children come as well, then their teachers should be present also.

When several teachers participate, the one in the centre should celebrate the Service itself, the one on the left reads the gospel and the one on the right does the communion. In this way all three would participate in the service.
A teacher (X): One pupil has asked me whether anything else might follow on from the Youth Service.
Dr Steiner: This is a question that has far-reaching significance. We must think more about this. We cannot do an actual mass. I would not like to bring in the mass. But something like the mass would be possible.
A teacher (X): We have been wondering about the relationship of the religion lessons to the movement for religious renewal. Some people think that the rituals belong to the Christian Community.
Dr Steiner: No one has ever maintained that the rituals for the school belong to the priests. The matter is as follows. The religion lessons are not given by the school but by the Anthroposophical Society. Side by side with these there are the Protestant and Catholic religion lessons. Some pupils might also attend the religion lessons of the Christian Community. This cannot be prevented. Perhaps we should ask ourselves what the Baptist community means to us. If some pupils insisted on going there,

we could do nothing about it. There is nothing we can do if some parents or children go there for religion lessons. But the arrangements we have made here stand in their own right.

The relationship of the Anthroposophical Society to the Christian Community will become a reality – it has always been clear in principle – when the moment arrives in which the Anthroposophical Society seeks to make things clear. The others are interested in the sense that they would like everyone to come to them. They have no reason to make things clear. But things must be made clear within the Anthroposophical Society. The principle followed here is, well, that the Anthroposophical Society exists, so we might as well be comfortable in it. You come in and sit down on the famous chairs and are comfortable. But what matters is how you do it. Things can only be clarified in reality if you are clear about them.

A teacher (Y): They are attempting to make things systematic and collect the rituals for all the sacraments.

Dr Steiner: The Christian Community is not our concern. I do not feel bound. If we do reach the point of adding something further after the Youth Service, I myself will give it. There is absolutely no need to wonder what will happen in connection with the Christian Community. They have their own rituals, and I have mentioned those rituals theoretically as something that might be possible. What are you worrying about? Let them worry if they want to. When he is here in the school, Pastor Ruhtenberg must entirely forget that he is a priest.* My activity [in connection with the Christian Community] has come to an end, with the exception of a few late additions. My activity was that of an adviser; I did not constitute or inaugurate. My activity ended on the final day spent by the ordained priests at Dornach. I did not ordain any priests. I showed how a priest is ordained.

---

* Wilhelm Ruhtenberg was a pastor who became a class teacher at the Waldorf School in Stuttgart in 1921, and soon became a teacher of the independent religious lessons. In 1922 he became a founding priest of theChristian Community, but continued working as a teacher for some years before taking up his priestly work with the Christian Community full time.

8. RELIGION LESSONS AND THE CHRISTIAN COMMUNITY

What happened was a self-ordination. The others were ordained by Dr Rittelmeyer. I do not maintain any kind of relationship with the Christian Community. This is a matter of principle. The Christian Community was to bring itself into being out of itself, and it has no connection in reality with the Anthroposophical Society. This matter, this standpoint, is as clear as anything can be. The others will not confuse the issue. They might confuse it by assuming that the Anthroposophical Society has certain rights.

When Herr Y brought up this matter, I said that I myself would engage the teachers. It is not a matter of my asking anybody about it. If the Christian Community for its part wants to recognize the religion teachers at the Waldorf School as their helpers, that is a matter for the Christian Community. If a teacher says that he is unconcerned about this, well, that is up to him. On the other hand the Christian Community is obliged to accept it if someone says he is not interested. This is how the matter stands in reality. The Christian Community has absolutely nothing to do with the Anthroposophical Society. It is in no way connected with the Anthroposophical Society. The Christian Community stands on its own. Its relationship with the Anthroposophical Society is no different from that of the Catholics or the Quakers.

Meeting of March 8, 1923

A religion teacher: Classes 8a and 8b are going to have the Youth Service. The children HR and LF want to be confirmed in the Christian Community, and their parents also wish it.

Dr Steiner: That is no concern of ours. Those who take part in our religion lessons can go to our Youth Service when they are old enough. But they could happen not to want to. But if they want to, why shouldn't they be allowed? If they want to go to both Youth Services we cannot stop them. There is anyway no fundamental difference. It doesn't concern us what they do there. In the Sunday Service, too, it finally comes down to whether the children want to take part or not. We can only leave the choice to them. We cannot insist, either, that they come to the Youth Service.

The question will solve itself. We can't discuss the matter. There is nothing to discuss with the independent religious movement. We can do as we wish and so can they. The children will then have it twice over. The way I see it is that we do not need to worry about it as it is a matter for the independent religious movement. We cannot forbid a father having his children confirmed there. Religion lessons are not compulsory. We cannot introduce Draconian measures. If we did, the children would not come. It is possible to allow someone to take part in the independent religion lessons without attending the Youth Service, but not the other way round. The girl can certainly take part in both religion lessons. Unless she participates in our religion lessons it would not be advisable for her to come to our Youth Service. Perhaps her father does not realise this. After all, it is her parents and not ourselves who are responsible.

A teacher: There is a girl who sometimes faints in the Sunday Service.

Dr Steiner: Let us do it twice, with half the number of children.

A teacher: The Offering Service is for Classes 10 and 11. Should Class 9 also go to it?

Dr Steiner: Yes, they can also go.

We shall take the two classes separately for the Youth Service, both times with Herr Uehli as the chief celebrant.

Meeting of June 19, 1924

A question is asked about religion lessons in the Waldorf School and in the Christian Community.

Dr Steiner: One thing should be considered. The Christian Community also gives religion lessons for children, doesn't it? Now we are constantly being asked, firstly, are the independent religion lessons in the Waldorf School compatible with the religion lessons in the Christian Community? And secondly, Is the Sunday Service at the school compatible with the Sunday

8. RELIGION LESSONS AND THE CHRISTIAN COMMUNITY

Service at the Christian Community? I would like to hear how you feel about this. First of all I should like to say, however, that if the children are managing satisfactorily in other respects, I have no real objection to their attending the religion lessons both at the Waldorf School and at the Christian Community and also attending both Services. The only impediment might possibly be one of health, in that it might be too much for them. But do say what you think. We do not want to make any dogmatic decisions.

The thing is this. We have seen the Christian Community develop out of the anthroposophical movement. There cannot possibly be any discrepancy between the two from the point of view of their content. The question of the religion lessons is a matter of principle with us to the extent that if the Christian Community claimed the right to teach the children who belong to them, we would have to grant them the same rights as the other denominations. In the independent religion lessons we shall no doubt always have the majority of the children who do not belong to the Christian Community. We would thus have one more type of religion lesson. But why should we make an issue of having Christian Community religion lessons in addition to the independent religion lessons? I really do not see how we could decide on the principle of the matter. For we cannot take the attitude of advising anyone not to take part in our own religion lessons. That would be a wrong thing to do.

Let us imagine a hypothetical case of a Catholic parent saying he wants to send his son not only to the Catholic religion lessons but also to the independent religion lessons. We could not object if it fitted in with the timetable. We cannot decide; it is the Christian Community that must decide.

[*Here is a gap in the shorthand report; and what follows is also not totally reliable.*]

... It is out of the question that at the Waldorf School a child should make a comparison and come to the conclusion that the religion lessons given by a Waldorf teacher are inferior. For in its inner nature the school is based on anthroposophy. Therefore if it should happen that a child makes a comparison between the teachers, then through the very nature of the case he would have to conclude that the Waldorf teacher is the better of the two.

A teacher asks about the choosing of new religion teachers.

Dr Steiner: You know, this fact could cause us greater difficulties some day than any we have so far had. You know how we have sweated blood to find religion teachers. The teachers here are occupied with their specialist subjects and there are of course certain conditions attached to the teaching of religion. We might be in the position some day of having to apply to the Christian Community for a religion teacher for the school. I should put that off as long as possible, but it might become necessary. I therefore cannot see at all why we should be so exclusive. We can leave it to the parents and children whether they take part both here and there. If they do go to both, I think the very best thing would be for the two religion teachers to discuss the subject matter, so that there is agreement.

You must also not ignore the fact that the priests of the Christian Community are among those anthroposophists who have made the greatest progress in the shortest time. The priests are not as they used to be, for they have made huge steps forward in inner development. The priests have made exemplary progress in their whole life of soul during the short time that the Christian Community has existed. Not all of them, of course, but by and large this is so, and they are bringing blessings in every field. In Breslau they had a meeting for young people run by two of the theologians. It was extremely productive. Young Wistinghausen is a blessing for the young people there.*

A teacher: How should we deal with newcomers? The children have already been confirmed in the Christian Community. Should they go straight into the Youth Service?

Dr Steiner: Yes, but it does not work out well. It would mean they would not be starting the Youth Service with an Easter festival. And

---

* Kurt von Wistinghausen (1901–86) one of the founding priests of the Christian Community, who worked in Breslau (now Wroclaw in Poland) at that time.

8. RELIGION LESSONS AND THE CHRISTIAN COMMUNITY

it is highly important that the Youth Service should begin with an Easter festival. So it would be best to assure them that they can join the Youth Service a little later on. You could let them be spectators, but not for a whole year. The Youth Service should come at Easter time when the children are at the end of Class 8. The whole Youth Service is orientated towards Easter, isn't it?

A teacher: How should we deal with the ones who have already had a Protestant confirmation?

Dr Steiner: In the first place it is principally a matter of the children having been confirmed. Then they take part in the independent religion lessons, and the whole meaning of the confirmation has gone. They negate it and expunge it from their lives. Someone who has been confirmed cannot simply go to the independent religion lessons. Being confirmed means being an active member of the Protestant Church. So you cannot take part in the independent religion lessons, for that would be denying one's confirmation. In the Catholic Church this is even worse. You would have to get over to the children tactfully that they must first of all live their way into what is new here. Then it will not seem such a bad thing if they do not take part in the Youth Service until the following Easter. You must first of all get them to realise that they would be 'forsaking' the old and turning to something quite different.

These things should be taken very seriously. If these seven children wait until Easter it could at the most be too early for them, but certainly not too late. We might reconsider the matter if one of them objects.

A question is asked.

Dr Steiner: I cannot in the least understand why someone who has been confirmed by priest K cannot be brought round to attending the Sunday Service for a year, since he has not attended it previously. In his case it can only be a question of attending the Sunday Service for a year.

If you take the inner significance of our Youth Service and the Youth Service [Confirmation] of the Christian Community you will find them compatible. The inner meaning of our Youth Service is that the human being is welcomed into humanity generally and not into a particular religious community. The Christian Community, however, welcomes them into a definite religious community. Inwardly these are absolutely compatible. If it is done in addition, there is no contradiction. But the other way round is not compatible. If they were confirmed there first, before coming to our Youth Service, that would be a contradiction. But not this way round. I have been asked by the Christian Community and by parents, can they have the Youth Service here first and then a kind of confirmation at the Christian Community. If a child has had the Youth Service here, we do not need to object. It is compatible, because it is not we who are welcoming the children into the Christian Community. I haven't said they *must* but that they *can* be confirmed in the Christian Community as well. Our Youth Service does not take the place of the Youth Service [Confirmation] at the Christian Community because it does not lead into the Christian Community. If they have been confirmed in the Christian Community they must wait, here, until next Easter.

A religion teacher says that the older pupils are no longer so willing to go to the Children's Service. They think they are now too old for it.

Dr Steiner: That is a totally wrong conception of the ritual. That is the Protestant view, which is to reject the ritual. It is possible to repeat the ritual throughout life. That is looking upon it as a teaching, as a preparation, not as a ritual. We must rid ourselves of this Protestant view.

References

1. Steiner, *Faculty Meetings with Rudolf Steiner*, meeting of Sep 26, 1919.
2. For instance in a lecture held in Cologne on March 17, 1905, 'Über die Bedeutung der Messe im Sinne der Mystik.' (Published in *Beiträge zur Rudolf Steiner Gesamtausgabe*, No. 110.)
3. Steiner, *Gospel of St John and its Relation to the Other Gospels*, lecture of July 7, 1909.
4. Steiner, *From Jesus to Christ*, lecture of Oct 13, 1911.
5. Steiner, *Anthroposophical Leading Thoughts*, pp.132–39.
6. Steiner, *The Spirit of the Waldorf School*, lecture of Sep 24, 1919.
7. Reprinted in *The Social Future*, February 1920. English translation included in *The Spirit of the Waldorf School*.
8. Schuster, Dr I. *Biblische Geschichten*, 1848. Most of this book was included in the Class 3 reader *Und Gott Sprach*, J.C. Mellinger Verlag, Stuttgart 1987.
9. Johann Peter Hebel (1760–1826), theologian and poet, *Die biblischen Geschichten*.
10. See Note 8.

Bibliography

Rittelmeyer, Friedrich, *Rudolf Steiner Enters My Life*, Floris Books, UK, 2013.

Steiner, Rudolf. Volume Nos refer to the Collected Works (CW), or to the German Gesamtausgabe (GA).

—, *Anthroposophical Leading Thoughts* (CW 26), Rudolf Steiner Press, UK 1973.

—, *Awakening to Community* (GA 257)

—, *Anthroposophic Press*, Spring Valley 1974.

—, *Calendar of the Soul*, The, Rudolf Steiner Press, UK 1963 (there are many other translations).

—, *Child's Changing Consciousness as the Basis of Pedagogical Practice*, The (CW 306) Anthroposophic Press, USA 1996.

—, *Discussions with Teachers* (CW 295), Anthroposophic Press, USA 1997.

—, *Education for Adolescents* (CW 302), Anthroposophic Press, USA 1996.

—, *Erziehung zum Leben: Selbsterziehung und pädagogische Praxis* (GA 297a) Dornach 1998.

—, *Essentials of Education*, The (CW 308) Anthroposophic Press, USA 1997.

—, *Faculty Meetings with Rudolf Steiner* (CW 300), 2 volumes, AP 1998 (previously published as *Rudolf Steiner's Conferences with the Teachers of the Waldorf School in Stuttgart*, 4 volumes Steiner Schools Fellowship Publications 1986–89.)

—, *From Jesus to Christ* (CW 131) Rudolf Steiner Press, UK 1991.

—, *Gospel of St John and its Relation to the Other Gospels*, The (CW 112) Anthroposophic Press, USA 1982.

—, *Human Values in Education* (CW 310), SteinerBooks, USA 2005.

—, *Kingdom of Childhood*, The (CW 311), Anthroposophic Press, USA 1995.

—, *Modern Art of Education*, A (GA 307) SteinerBooks, USA 2004.
—, *Philosophy, Cosmology and Religion* (CW 215) Anthroposophic Press, USA 1984.
—, *Practical Advice to Teachers* (GA 294), SteinerBooks, USA 2000.
—, *Renewal of Education through the Science of the Spirit*, The (CW 301) SteinerBooks, USA 2001 (previously published by Steiner Schools Fellowship, Forest Row, 1989).
—, *Roots of Education*, The (CW 309) Anthroposophic Press, USA 1997.
—, *Soul Economy: Body, Soul, and Spirit in Waldorf Education* (CW 303) SteinerBooks, USA 2003 (previously published as *Soul Economy and Waldorf Education*, Anthroposophic Press, USA & Rudolf Steiner Press, UK 1986).
—, *Spirit of the Waldorf School*, The (CW 297), Anthroposophic Press, USA 1996.
—, *Spiritual Ground of Education*, The (GA 305) SteinerBooks, USA 2004.
—, Anthroposophical Publishing Co., London 1947.
—, *Supersensible Knowledge as a Demand of the Age. Anthroposophy and the Ethical-Religious Conduct of Life* (part of CW 84) Anthroposophic Press, New York & Rudolf Steiner Publishing Co., 1943.
—, *Theosophy* (GA 9), Anthroposophic Press, New York 1994.
—, *Verantwortung des Menschen für die Weltentwickelung, Die* (GA 203) Dornach 1978.
—, *Waldorf Education and Anthroposophy* (CW 304) Anthroposophic Press, USA 1995.

More books from the Steiner Waldorf Schools Fellowship

The Care and Development of the Human Senses
Willi Aeppli

*The Educational Tasks and Content of the
Steiner Waldorf Curriculum*
edited by Martyn Rawson, Tobias Richter and Kevin Avison

Educating through Arts and Crafts
edited by Michael Martin

Five Plays for Waldorf Festivals
Richard Moore

A Handbook for Waldorf Class Teachers
edited by Kevin Avison

Language Teaching in Steiner Waldorf Schools
Johnannes Kiersch

Report Verses in Rudolf Steiner's Art of Education
Heinz Müller

Republican Academies
Francis Gladstone

Rudolf Steiner's Curriculum for Waldorf Schools
E. A. Karl Stockmeyer

Three Lectures on the Curriculum of the Waldorf School
Rudolf Steiner

Towards Creative Teaching

Notes to an Evolving Curriculum for Steiner Waldorf Class Teachers

edited by Martyn Rawson and Kevin Avison

This wonderful resource book for Steiner-Waldorf class teachers offers ideas for planning, shaping and developing lessons for Classes 1 to 8.

Taking the Waldorf curriculum as its basis, and without being restrictive or prescriptive, this book comes out of a teachers' working group and provides helpful suggestions to both class teachers and subject specialists, adding to the richness and imagination of each teacher's own work.

The book is a truly comprehensive overview of all main-lesson and accompanying subjects, offering a wealth of guidance, knowledge and inspiration for Waldorf class teachers.

www.florisbooks.co.uk

The Care and Development of the Human Senses

Rudolf Steiner's work on the significance of the senses in education

Willi Aeppli

An in-depth presentation of Steiner's ideas about the nature of the twelve human senses, as he saw them, and their role in education.

Of interest to teachers and parents of students attending Steiner-Waldorf institutions, this book is also written for anyone with an interest in children's education and philosophies of teaching.

www.florisbooks.co.uk